PERSPECTIVES
on
PENTECOST

PERSPECTIVES

on

PENTECOST

Studies in New Testament Teaching
on the Gifts of the Holy Spirit

RICHARD B. GAFFIN, JR.

Presbyterian and Reformed
Publishing Company
Phillipsburg, New Jersey

Printed in the United States of America

Preface

This volume began as a series of lectures given throughout New Zealand under the auspices of the Evangelical Reformed Conferences in December 1974–January 1975. They subsequently served as the basis for a study paper prepared for a conference on the work of the Holy Spirit held in connection with the meeting of the Reformed Ecumenical Synod in Cape Town, South Africa, in August 1976. This paper, in turn, was expanded into a course of twelve lectures given at Westminster Theological Seminary during the winter term, January 1977. Along the way I have valued the (sometimes sharp) criticisms that have been raised, and I hope that what is written here reflects a measure of benefit from them all.

When quoting from Scripture I have followed the practice of choosing from among the various standard translations or providing one of my own. The translations cited by abbreviation are the following:

KJV (King James Version)
NASB (New American Standard Bible)
NEB (The New English Bible)
NIV (New International Version-New Testament)
RSV (Revised Standard Version)

My thanks to Mrs. Betty Stevenson and Mrs. Mary Koll Martin for typing the manuscript, and to the Board of Trustees of

Westminster Theological Seminary for a leave of absence during
the first semester and winter term, 1977–78, in part to work on
this volume.

Westminster Theological Seminary
June 1978

Contents

I

A Promise and a Plea

Controversy in the church is both distressing and hopeful. It is distressing because it is essentially counterproductive, an abnormality which, to mention only one set of consequences, compromises the church, reduces its credibility both to itself and the world, and thus impairs its effectiveness in the world. But unlike controversy in the world, which at best softens into uneasy compromises, controversy in the church holds the promise of constructive resolution, especially where the different sides are able to recognize in one another a common commitment to the final authority of the Bible as God's Word. Where the controversy itself, at least in its best moments, reflects the effort of wrestling with the meaning of Scripture in order to be more fully obedient to the Lord, then there is hope for genuine unity in the truth.

Since around 1960 few topics have received more attention in the church than the gifts of the Holy Spirit. Some would say that this is still today *the* issue confronting the worldwide church. Certainly none has been the occasion of greater controversy and division within the church. That controversy is intense. Differences are strongly felt and often sharply expressed, and this is understandable, because at stake is Christian practice, the very personal experience of being a Christian.

This book is yet another entry into this highly-charged controversy over the gifts of the Spirit. Like many others it too reflects

II

The Gift of the Spirit

A brief survey of overall New Testament teaching on the work of the Holy Spirit will benefit an examination of any one aspect like the gifts of the Spirit. Such a survey to identify controlling perspectives and themes can be done from a number of angles. The approach chosen here especially serves an interest in the question of spiritual gifts.

Even a superficial glance at the New Testament with a concordance in hand discloses an unmistakable pattern. The great majority of references to the Holy Spirit are found in the last half of the New Testament. Approximately 80 percent are in Acts, the Epistles and Revelation, with only a relative handful in the Gospels. More significant is the nature of this distribution of references. In the Gospels, so far as the present work of the Spirit is concerned, the accent is on Jesus and his activity. For the disciples, the Spirit is largely a matter of *promise*, a still *future* gift. In Acts and the Epistles, however, emphasis is on the *present* reality of the Spirit as he is active in the church and at work in believers. This pattern raises a key question: what explains this difference, this decisive transition for the disciples? The answer, of course, is Pentecost, which can be variously described as the baptism of (in, with) the Holy Spirit, or the outpouring, or the gift, of the Holy Spirit.[1]

---

1. The interchangeability of these expressions applied to Pentecost is clear from Acts 1:5; cf. 11:16 (baptism); 2:17, 18, 33; 10:45 (outpouring); 2:38; 10:45; 11:17; 15:8 (gift, giving). Cf. the use of still other verbal notions: "coming on" (Acts 1:8), "filling" (2:4), "receiving" (2:38; 10:47), "falling upon" (11:15; cf. 10:44).

The New Testament, then, provides a dramatic, historical perspective basic to understanding the work of the Spirit. It is fair to say that everything said in the New Testament about the Spirit's work looks forward or traces back to Pentecost; everything pivots on Pentecost (along with the death and resurrection of Christ). Accordingly, a question for reflection is what really happened at Pentecost. What is the significance of the gift (baptism) of the Holy Spirit? Basic answers lie along two major, closely interrelated lines: (A) Pentecost and Christ and (B) Pentecost and the church, from which follow implications for (C) Pentecost and the experience of the individual believer.

A. Pentecost and Christ (the christological dimension)

At Pentecost it is Jesus who baptizes with the Holy Spirit. In fact, the work of Christ in its entirety may be said to consist in securing and communicating to the church at Pentecost the gift (baptism) of the Holy Spirit. This fundamental thesis can be developed and better appreciated from the twin angles of (1) promise and (2) fulfillment.

1. Noteworthy is the way in which all four Gospels record the preparatory ministry and proclamation of John the Baptist, in particular the contrast John draws between himself and the coming Messiah. His witness in the unit John 1:29–34 is that the work of Jesus, as "the Lamb of God, who takes away the sin of the world" (v. 29), and "the Son of God" (v. 34), climaxes and focuses in the fact that, while John has been sent to baptize with water (vv. 31, 33), Jesus is "the one who baptizes with the Holy Spirit" (v. 33).
The Synoptics provide a similar profile:

> The people were waiting expectantly and were all wondering in their hearts if John might possibly be the Christ. John answered them all, "I baptize you with water. But one more powerful than I will come, the thongs of whose sandals I am not worthy to untie. He will baptize you with the Holy Spirit and fire. His winnowing fork is in his hand to clear his threshing floor and to gather the wheat into his barn, but he will burn up the chaff with

unquenchable fire." And with many other words John exhorted
the people and preached the good news to them. (Luke 3:15–18,
NIV; cf. Matt. 3:11f.; Mark 1:7f.)

Pressed by the crowd to identify himself, particularly whether
he might be the Messiah (v. 15), John responds by meeting this
question at the basic level on which it was asked and in terms of
the sweeping perspectives it opened up. His answer (vv. 16f.)
briefly summarizes his ministry and that of Jesus, the "coming
one," by comparing them in terms of the common denominator of
baptism: John's role is provisional and preparatory, his call to
repentance is anticipatory (cf. v. 4; 7:27f.); therefore his ministry
in its entirety is set under the sign of water baptism. In contrast,
Jesus is the fulfillment; therefore his ministry taken as a whole
consists in the reality of baptism with the Holy Spirit and fire.

Verse 17 plainly shows that the fire of the Messiah's baptism is
destructive, or at least includes a destructive aspect (cf. v. 9), and
that this baptism as a whole involves nothing less than the eschatological judgment with its dual outcome of salvation or destruction. Messianic Spirit-and-fire baptism is of a piece with
God's great discriminating activity of cleansing the world-
threshing floor or, to vary the metaphor slightly, harvesting the
world-field, at the end of history (cf. Jesus' explanation of the
parable of the weeds, Matt. 13:36–43).

This point, the eschatological significance of the Messiah's baptism with the Holy Spirit and fire, is fundamental not only for
understanding Pentecost but also the intervening Lucan gospel
narrative in its entirety. Luke is concerned to show that, contrary
apparently even to John's expectations (Luke 7:18ff.), the promised messianic baptism does not ensue immediately but is pre-
ceded by a period based on Jesus' own submission to John's water
baptism and correlative reception of the Spirit (Luke 3:21f.; note
an almost identical structure in Matthew 3:13–17 and Mark 1:9–
11, in which the account of Jesus' baptism follows directly on
John's prophecy). For the Spirit-and-fire baptism, eventually
realized at Pentecost, to be one of blessing rather than destruction
for the messianic people, the Messiah himself must first become
identified with them as their representative sin-bearer (the point

of Jesus' being baptized by John, from which John recoils; cf. Matt. 3:14) and be endowed with the Spirit, in order to bear away the wrath and condemnation of God their sins deserve. If they are to receive the Spirit as a gift and blessing, then he must receive the Spirit for the task of removing the curse on them.

This close integration of John's ministry and baptism, Jesus' own reception of the Spirit, and Pentecost is pointedly expressed in John 1:33. Identifying Jesus in his role as "the Lamb of God, who takes away the sin of the world" (v. 29), the Baptist says that he would not have known him (as such), "except that the one who sent me to baptize with water told me, 'The man on whom you see the Spirit come down and remain is he who will baptize with the Holy Spirit.' "

Jesus' own declaration in Luke 12:49–51 also serves to clarify the overall picture: "I have come to bring fire on the earth, and how I wish it were already kindled! I have a baptism to undergo, and how distressed I am until the ordeal is over! Do you suppose I came to bring peace on earth? No indeed, I have come to bring division" (cf. Mark 10:38f.). The echo of themes central in Luke 3:16b, 17 is unmistakable: destructive fire, baptism, both set in the context of differentiating judgment. This provides further support for understanding the references to baptism in 3:15ff. as references to judgment, either as the sign (John's water baptism, including Jesus' own baptism by John) or the reality (Spirit-and-fire baptism). It also warrants viewing the entirety of Jesus' ministry, certainly its climax in his death, as a baptism ordeal, understood as his own enduring of the eschatological judgment (condemnation) in view in John's prophecy of messianic baptism.

2. The centrality of Pentecost in the work of Christ is no less apparent from the perspective of fulfillment.

a. Peter's sermon on the day of Pentecost (Acts 2:14–39) is basically Christ-centered. Peter explains the coming of the Spirit by preaching Christ. The pivot of much that he says is found in verses 32 and 33. Having dwelt on the resurrection (v. 24–31) as God's response to the wicked men who crucified Christ (v. 23), Peter summarizes by saying: "God has raised up this Jesus, to which we are all witnesses. Therefore having been exalted to the right hand of God, and having received from the Father the promise of the Holy Spirit [i.e., the promised Holy Spirit], he has poured out what you both see and hear." The outpouring of the Spirit as *the* promise of the Father (cf. 1:4; Luke 24:49), and so the essence of the entire fulfillment awaited under the old covenant (Acts 2:39; cf. Gal. 3:14; Eph. 1:13), is here seen to be closely connected with the epochal, climactic events of Christ's work, especially his resurrection and ascension. Together with these other events Pentecost is part of a single, unified complex of events and is epochal on the order that they are. In their mutual once-for-all significance the one event could not have occurred without the others.

Further, particularly within the overall structure of Luke-Acts where the tie between John's water baptism and Holy Spirit baptism is made plain (cf. in addition to the discussion above the explicit linking of the two by Jesus in Acts 1:5), the movement of thought here suggests a parallel between Jesus' own baptism by John and Pentecost that is difficult to evade: At the Jordan, the Spirit was given to Jesus, by the Father (Luke 3:22), as endowment for the messianic task before him, in order that he might accomplish the salvation of the church; at Pentecost, the Spirit, received by Jesus, from the Father, as reward for the redemptive work finished and behind him, was given by him to the church as the (promised) gift (of the Father). The fully trinitarian complexion of Pentecost is plain.

In order to keep the larger picture in view, we should note that the preceding discussion of Luke-Acts involves the conclusion that the "already-not yet" structure of New Testament eschatology as a whole also applies to the fulfillment of John's prophecy in Luke 3:16, 17. Its undeniable fulfillment at Pentecost is nonetheless component with the fiery baptism of final judgment set by the New Testament to be executed by Christ at his return (e.g., Matt. 16:27; Acts 10:42; 17:31; II Thess. 1:7f.; II Tim. 4:1).

Also, while the accent in the Pentecost fulfillment is no doubt on the Holy Spirit as blessing, the presence of the fire in the form of tongues resting on each one present (Acts 2:3) should not be forgotten. Without trying to settle the question here, this phenomenon should be understood against the backdrop of John's prophecy, either as indicating that the baptismal fire of destructive judgment has been exhausted in the case of the church and will not consume it, or as signifying the refining, purifying aspect of the Spirit's work in the church (for the latter alternative, see especially Mal. 3:1–3).

b. Paul's frequently overlooked commentary in this connection is I Corinthians 15:45 (cf. II Cor. 3:17). In the larger context of the whole chapter he asserts and discusses, over against those who deny it, the future bodily resurrection of believers. The controlling motif, running like a thread through his entire argument, is the unity of the resurrection of Christ and believers. This solidarity in the experience of resurrection is expressed most pointedly in verse 20: Christ's resurrection is the "firstfruits" of the great resurrection-harvest. What God has done for Christ, he will also do for believers (cf. Rom. 8:11).

The immediate context (vv. 42–49) is concerned with the nature of the resurrection body identified in verse 44a as a "spiritual body." In this respect the point of verse 45 is that Christ, as resurrected, is the model of and the first to have received the spiritual body believers will receive at their resurrection (cf. v. 49b; Rom. 8:29). Verse 45, however, says much more about Christ than that he is an exemplar, the first in a series. As resurrected and ascended (cf. the correlative references to "heaven" and "heavenly" in vv. 47–49), he has become "life-giving Spirit."

Three sets of remarks bear on the understanding of this remarkable statement. (1) In my judgment there can be little doubt in view of Paul's usage in I Corinthians 2:10ff. (especially vv. 13f.) and II Corinthians 3:3ff. (especially v. 6) as well as his almost invariable use of the adjective *spiritual* (e.g., Rom. 1:11; I Cor. 12:1; Gal. 6:1; Eph. 1:3; Col. 1:9) that πνευματικόν in I Corinthians 15:44 and 46 and πνεῦμα in verse 45 refer to the activity and person of the Holy Spirit, respectively. (2) In saying that Christ is life-giving Spirit in the sense of the Holy Spirit, Paul is not introducing trinitarian confusion. Essential, eternal, innertrinitarian relationships are outside his purview here. Rather his perspective is *historical*. He is speaking about what Christ *became* in his identity as the last *Adam* and second *man* (v. 47). The oneness or unity in view is economic, functional, eschatological. Paul's point is that by virtue of his exaltation (resurrection and ascension) Christ, as last Adam and second man, has come into such permanent and complete possession of the Spirit that the two are equated in their *activity*. The two are seen as one, as they have been *made* one in the eschatological *work* of giving life to the church, that life which has its visible "firstfruits" in Christ's own resurrection. (3) While the life-giving work in view in this passage is primarily that of the future bodily resurrection of believers at the parousia, at the same time surely who Christ is and what he does *presently* by virtue of his resurrection is also in view.

c. Weaving together this perspective of Paul with Peter's Pentecost sermon, we may say not only that at Pentecost Christ pours out on the church the gift of the Spirit but also that Pentecost is Christ's personal coming to the church as the life-giving Spirit. The Spirit of Pentecost is the resurrection life of Christ, the life of the exalted Christ.

This is enforced by what Jesus himself has to say to his disciples in John 14–16, when he promises the coming of the Spirit as Paraclete (Counselor, Comforter). In particular, at 14:12ff. the point is made that the giving of the Spirit (the other Paraclete, v. 16) by the Father both is conditioned on Jesus' *going* to the Father (v. 12) in his glorification (death, resurrection, and ascension), and at the same time is the *coming* of Jesus himself (v. 18: "I will not leave you as orphans; I will come to you"). Jesus' further promises of his presence and coming in verses 19–23 ought similarly to be understood of the coming of the Spirit, rather than as referring either to the brief period of his postresurrection appearances or the second coming.

Emerging in our discussion, then, is one of the most basic, controlling principles of both the christology and the pneumatology of the New Testament, namely, the absolute coalescence, the total congruence in the church between the work of the exalted Christ and the work of the Holy Spirit. The work of the Spirit is not some addendum to the work of Christ. It is not some more or less independent sphere of activity that goes beyond or supplements what Christ has done. The Spirit's work is not a "bonus" added to the basic salvation secured by Christ. Rather the coming of the Spirit brings to light not only that Christ *has* lived and *has* done certain things but that he, as the source of eschatological life, *now* lives and is at work in the church. By and in the Spirit Christ reveals himself as present. The Spirit is the powerfully open secret, the revealed mystery, of Christ's abiding presence in the church.

So, for example, the familiar words of Christ at the close of the Great Commission—"I am with you always, even to the end of the age" (Matt. 28:20)—are not to be understood only in terms of Christ's omnipresence by virtue of his divine nature, but also and perhaps primarily in terms of the presence and activity of the Spirit. The "I" who speaks here is the life-giving Spirit, the glorified Son of Man, about to come and be present in the church through the power of the Spirit.

Conclusion: Viewed from the angle of Christ's person and work, Pentecost means that the Spirit is now present and active in the covenant community on the basis, and as the climax, of the finished redemptive accomplishment of Christ. This is the perspective and the sense of the interpretive comment of the evangelist in John 7:39: "The Spirit had not yet been given, because Jesus was not yet glorified."

Further, the gift of the Spirit is nothing less than the gift of Christ himself to the church, the Christ who has become what he is by virtue of his sufferings, death, and exaltation. In this sense the gift (baptism, outpouring) of the Spirit is the crowning achievement of Christ's work. It is his coming in exaltation to the church in the power of the Spirit. It completes the once-for-all accomplishment of salvation. It is the apex thus far reached in the unfolding of redemptive history. Without it, the work that climaxes in Christ's death and resurrection would be unfinished, incomplete.

B. Pentecost and the Church (the ecclesiological dimension)

It should be apparent that we have been discussing Pentecost and the church all along. Again and again in speaking of Pentecost in relation to Christ it has not only been natural but necessary to mention the church. This happens, of course, because the work of Christ is never private, merely for himself, but always messianic, for and in the interests of the church. A christological perspective and an ecclesiological perspective are closely complementary and inevitably intertwine. Consequently, while this dimension could be discussed extensively, I limit myself here for the most part to spelling out briefly several conclusions especially pertinent to the question of spiritual gifts.

Pentecost is nothing less than the establishment of the church as the new covenant people of God, as the body of Christ. The Spirit given at Pentecost constitutes the body of Christ as a dwelling place of God in the Spirit (Eph. 2:22), as the temple of God in which the Spirit of God dwells (I Cor. 3:16). Accordingly, all who have been incorporated into that Spirit-baptized body and have a place in it share in the gift of the Spirit (I Cor. 12:13).

This blending of christological, pneumatological and ecclesiological considerations, in particular the interchangeability of Christ and the Spirit in the experience of the church, is nowhere more plain than in Romans 8:9, 10: those who "belong to Christ" (v. 9d, i.e., are "in Christ") are at the same time those "in the Spirit" (v. 9a), those in whom "the Spirit of God dwells" (the Spirit in you, v. 9b), and those in whom Christ dwells ("Christ in you," v. 10a), all because of, to emphasize it again, who the Spirit is (the Spirit of Christ—v. 9c), and who Christ is (the life-giving Spirit—I Cor. 15:45). The issue here is not only the inseparable conjunction of Christ and the Spirit in the experience of believers, but also the constitutive grounding of this conjunction *in back of* and *prior to* our experience, in what took place once for all in the experience of Christ, in the definitive, once-for-all accomplishment of our salvation.

The gift of the Spirit in which all in the church share, embracing all the differences in individual outworkings of this gift, is described by Paul as the "down payment," "pledge" (II Cor. 1:22; 5:5; Eph. 1:14) and "firstfruits" (Rom. 8:23) of the full inheritance to be received at Christ's return. These terms function pointedly to express at the same time both the *partial, anticipatory* nature of the church's present possession of the Spirit, and the *eschatological* character of this gift and of those activities of the Spirit presently experienced by *all* within the church. The further significance of this point will concern us below.

C. Pentecost and the Individual Believer
(the experiential dimension)

1. Perhaps by now it is clear that what happened at Pentecost was not first of all or basically a matter of the special, striking experience of the 120 Christians there. Even less is it the model for a postconversion, second-blessing experience of the Spirit to be sought by all believers in every generation of the church. Here we find ourselves at odds with a viewpoint that has had great influence and is still widely held, both in the older Pentecostal denominations and the present charismatic movement.[2] We ought, then, to give some attention to it for the bearing it has on the subject of spiritual gifts.

The controlling point in the position taken here is that Pentecost is to be understood first of all as part of the once-for-all accomplishment of redemption (*historia salutis*) rather than as a part of its ongoing, continual application (*ordo salutis*). Obviously the two are intimately related and inseparable, but they must not be confused. To do so necessarily jeopardizes the absolute sufficiency and finality of Christ's work. As I have already tried to show, the baptism with the Holy Spirit at Pentecost is a unique event of epochal significance in the history of redemption. Therefore it is no more capable of being repeated or serving as a model for individual Christian experience than are the death, resurrection and ascension of Christ, with which it is so integrally conjoined as part of a single complex of events (see again Acts 2:32f.).

The events recorded in Acts 8:14ff., 10:44ff. (11:15–18), and 19:1ff. are typically appealed to as refuting this conclusion and as warranting some sort of second-blessing doctrine. Some attention, then, needs to be given these passages here. This will be done in a way which does skirt some of the thorny exegetical problems they

---

2. I have the impression that this view may be on the decline, at least in some sectors of the charismatic movement, the reason being that as an increasing number of serious efforts are made to support and defend it exegetically, the difficulties of doing so become more and more apparent. But this assessment may be wrong.

present but is, I hope, responsible and does not ignore any aspect of their bearing on the issues we have raised.

Of first importance, hardly capable of being overemphasized, is a general hermeneutical consideration concerning the way Acts is to be read. If, as is too often the case, Acts is read primarily as more or less random samplings of earliest Christian piety and practice, as a compilation of illustrations taken from the early history and experience of the church—a more or less loose collection of edifying and inspiring episodes, usually with the nuance that they are from the "good old days, when Christians were really Christians"—then we will tend to become preoccupied with the experience of particular individuals and groups recorded there, to idealize that experience, and to try to recapture it for ourselves. But if, as ought to be the case, Acts is read with an eye for its careful overall composition and what we will presently see is one of Luke's central purposes in writing, then these passages and the experiences they record come into proper focus.

Specifically, one of Luke's purposes is to document the foundational (i.e., *apostolic*) spread of the gospel from Israel to the nations. He is intent on recording the initial, once-for-all establishment of the new covenant church as made up of both Jew and Gentile, through the ministry of the apostles and those associated with them. Acts is to be read in the light of Jesus' promise and statement of program to the apostles in 1:8, which has as good a claim as any to being the theme verse of Acts: "But you will receive power when the Holy Spirit comes on you; and you will be my witnesses in Jerusalem, and in all Judea and Samaria, and to the ends of the earth" (NIV). The subsequent narrative in Acts as a whole conforms broadly to the pattern indicated here: Jerusalem-Judea-Samaria-the ends of earth (Rome at the other end of the Mediterranean world). Luke is concerned to show that subsequent developments transpired as Jesus promised they would.

It needs to be stressed that Acts 1:8 is not addressed indiscriminately to all believers, regardless of time and place, but directly only to the *apostles* (cf. v. 2 where the "you" of v. 8 is explicitly identified as the apostles), and concerns the foundational task of bringing the gospel from Jerusalem to Rome *completed* by them (cf. Col. 1:6, 23). It does apply today, but only derivatively, as we build on the apostolic foundation and hold fast to their foundational gospel witness. Where this is not grasped, one result is an unintentional, but common, misuse of the verse. Most assuredly the local congregation, or any other larger or smaller locale in the Western world serving as a base for contemporary missionary activity, is not "Jerusalem"! Rather we today are part of "the ends of the earth" reached by the gospel in the period beyond its foundational spread.

The events recorded in Acts 8, 10 (11), and 19, then, together with the striking occurrences they involve (note, however, that there is no mention of tongues in chap. 8), are not repetitions of what took place at Pentecost as parts of a series to continue indefinitely. Rather they are elements in the initial, foundational spread of the gospel and so correlate with the events of Acts 2 as parts of a unique, nonrepeatable (i.e., nontypical, nonmodular) complex of events.

To grasp the reality involved, we may say that these events are extensions of Pentecost, parts of the expansion or spreading of the scope of the baptism with the Spirit, or the fulfillment of the Pentecost-promise in stages or installments, but always with the proviso that "extensions," "expansions," "stages," etc., are determined by and restricted in their usage to what took place once for all through the foundational ministry of the apostles.

This approach to these verses is partially dependent on what will be said in addition below about the apostles and the foundational nature of their ministry (pp. 89–93). For the present we go on here to note several supporting indications in the passages themselves. The point I want especially to underscore is that in none of them is the focus or primary attention on the experience of individual believers as such. The profile in chapter 8 is that the events described there (vv. 14ff.) take place and have their significance in view of the fact that "the *apostles* in *Jerusalem* had heard that *Samaria* had received the word of God" (v. 14). In chapter 10 (11) what took place in the household of Cornelius is significant because "the *apostles* and the brethren who were throughout *Judea* heard that the *Gentiles* also had received the word of God" (11:1; note the structural similarities with the statement of 8:14), and because the *Gentiles* had been given the gift of the Holy Spirit (10:45; 11:15–18; 15:7f.; note, not as a postconversion experience, but in view of "repentance unto life," 11:18).

Acts 19:1–7 contains a number of perplexities. But whatever may be their full understanding or the precise reference of "disciples" in verse 1, the sense of the passage pivots on the specific historical qualification that these men lived at the time of John the Baptist and had been directly involved with his ministry and movement. The significance of the incident depends on the fact that they had received John's baptism (v. 3), that is, that they had at one time been his disciples.

What takes place, then, in their encounter with Paul is with a view to removing the unusual, indeed anomalous, situation of those who have responded to the ministry of John and received the sign of his water baptism but have not learned of or been involved in the reality of the fulfillment in Jesus, to which John's ministry with its baptism sign pointed. Paul's primary concern is to proclaim this reality with its implications for Christian discipleship (vv. 4ff.). At any rate, the right interpretation of this passage must confront the specific redemptive-historical delimitation involved.[3]

2. All that has so far been said is not intended to deny or minimize the reality of the experiences recorded in Acts 2 and the other passages just discussed. Those experiences, however, are qualified by the following considerations:

a. Their "dispensational," once-for-all character is not difficult to see. The experience of those involved at Pentecost, for example, happens to be postconversion for *them*, because their experience as a whole is unique. They were the generation living when "the fulness of time came" (Gal. 4:4), when redemptive history (*his-*

---

3. In view of the baptismal contact of these men with John as well as the pointed and explicit connection the latter drew between his water baptism and impending Holy Spirit-and-fire baptism (Luke 3:16), it is difficult to avoid translating verse 2: "No, we have not even heard that the Holy Spirit has been given." An unfortunate development in this respect occurs in the NIV, which in its first printing (1973) reads as just given, but in all impressions since 1974, without any explanation in the margin or elsewhere so far as I can discover, reverts to the rendering: "No, we have not even heard that there is a Holy Spirit."

toria salutis) reached its once-for-all consummation in Christ. The attempt to read out of Acts 2 and the other passages a permanent model (*ordo salutis*) for receiving the Spirit creates a number of unanswerable questions: Does "Holy Spirit baptism" take place at the same time as or subsequent to initial faith in Christ? The former is the case in chapter 10 and perhaps (but not indisputably) chapter 19, the latter in chapters 2 and 8. Before or after water baptism? The former in chapter 10, the latter in chapters 8 and 19, with chapter 2 giving no indication. With or without laying on hands? The former in chapters 8 and 19, the latter in chapters 2 and 10. These dilemmas simply show that the passages in question are being pressed into doing something Luke never intended.

The resurrection, ascension, and Pentecost, particularly the first, had an undeniably crucial impact on the disciples, involving nothing less than a "heart inflaming," "mind opening" transformation (Luke 24:32, 45) in their understanding of Jesus' person and work and their commitment to him. And in a sense it can also be said that there were no "Christians" before Pentecost (see the comments above on Pentecost as the founding of the New Testament church). Still the position sometimes taken that Acts 2 and 8 describe the conversion of those present is beset with substantial difficulties. Most decisive is Peter's preresurrection confession: "You are the Christ, the Son of the living God" (Matt. 16:16; cf. Mark 8:29; Luke 9:20), a confession for which Jesus pronounces him "blessed" because "it was not revealed to you by man but by my Father in heaven" (v. 17). Again: "Lord, to whom shall we go? You have the words of eternal life. We believe and know that you are the Holy One of God" (John 6:68f., NIV). This heartfelt, Spirit-worked confession, presumably not unique to Peter among the disciples (cf. Matt. 16:20), can only be heard as reflecting the saving, justifying faith of which Abraham has all along been the model (Rom. 4; Gal. 3:6ff.), and so as reflecting Peter's conversion in the sense of his saving incorporation into the covenant community. Accordingly, when in recalling Pentecost Peter says: "If God gave them [the Gentiles] the same gift as he gave us when we believed in the Lord Jesus Christ . . ." (Acts 11:17), it is surely gratuitous to insist that he is referring to his initial act of saving faith. Rather,

there is an intimation here of the fact that at every point in the
believer's life, faith functions to receive what God has to give.
Acts 8 does present some perplexities that are difficult to re-
solve (e.g., is the faith of Simon reported in v. 13 genuine or not?).
It is not necessary to do so, however, in order to challenge the
view that the Samaritans were not converted until the events described in verses 14ff. One large difficulty with this position is
verse 14, where Luke's summary of what had already taken place
(vv. 5–13) is that "Samaria had received the word of God." A
virtually identical summary expression occurs in 11:1 (". . . the
Gentiles had also received the word of God"). Since the latter
instance obviously refers to the unquestionably genuine conversion of the Gentiles, it seems best to give Acts 8:14 the same force
and so to conclude that the experience described in verses 14 and
15, like that in Acts 2, is postconversion.

   b. The experiential significance of Pentecost for the disciples
ought to be measured, among other considerations, by the note on
which Luke chooses to end his Gospel (24:53): "They were continually in the temple, praising God." It seems fair to suggest (1)
that the content of the praise ascribed here to the disciples was
focused in their new heart-inflaming, mind-opening insight (vv.
32, 45) into the true significance of Christ's death and resurrection. The content of their praise, in other words, was the gospel
with its center in the cross and resurrection. (2) "In the temple"
shows this praise to have been in some respect public or at least
not deliberately secluded. (3) "Continually" (διὰ παντὸς) points to
their praise as a characteristic, persistent, perhaps even absorbing
activity. The conclusion, then, is that Luke intimates a transforming experience for the disciples, after the resurrection and before
Pentecost, resulting in open, positive gospel witness.

   Without putting an exaggerated stress on this (frequently overlooked) statement or denying the powerful impact of Pentecost on
the disciples personally, it does seem required to modify the
widespread notion that Pentecost has its primary significance as
the empowering experience transforming the disciples (e.g., Peter) from cowering timidity to unshakable boldness. This recognition, in turn, suggests a shift in accent away from preoccupation

with the experiential significance of Pentecost (which tends to lead down a wrong track) to the christological and ecclesiological perspectives already discussed above.

c. It is important to distinguish the phenomena experienced at Pentecost and elsewhere (e.g., wind, fire, tongues-speaking) from the gift of the Spirit. The gift of the Spirit is the exalted Christ himself, the life-giving Spirit, present in the church in the fulness of his working. The phenomena, while specific manifestations of that gift on particular occasions, are not to be identified with it nor even viewed as its invariable accompaniment. The gift of the Spirit ought not to be defined in terms of these phenomena.

3. The expression, "to baptize in" or "with the (one) (Holy) Spirit"—βαπτίζω ἐν (ἑνὶ) πνεύματι (ἁγίῳ)—occurs seven times in the New Testament. Six of these refer specifically to Pentecost or, more accurately, to the once-for-all Pentecost event-complex analyzed above (Matt. 3:11; Mark 1:8; Luke 3:16; John 1:33; Acts 1:5; 11:16). The seventh, in I Corinthians 12:13, is fairly taken as addressed to the situation of believers (like the church today) who were not present at Pentecost or the associated epochal events recorded in Acts. It relates Pentecost (Holy Spirit baptism, the gift of the Spirit) to their *experience*. It instructs us on the place of baptism with the Spirit in the ongoing *application* of redemption (*ordo salutis*).

Large in the context of chapter 12 is Paul's interest in the work of the Spirit, particularly the variety of spiritual gifts (which ought to be) functioning in the congregation. A deeper, more fundamental consideration, however, explicitly controls all he has to say, namely, the church as the body of Christ (especially vv. 12–27). In the case of the Spirit, Paul's overall emphasis is on the harmonious balance between unity and diversity: the one Spirit and his many gifts (vv. 4–11, especially 4 and 11). But all Paul says about the activity of the Spirit is rooted in the more basic reality that the church, as the body of Christ, is the *locus*, the place where the Spirit is present in his diverse working. The variety of the *one* Spirit's work is an expression or function of the *one* body with its various and organically, harmoniously interacting parts (v. 12).

The preposition ἐν (v. 13a) is frequently given an instrumental force ("by one Spirit we were all baptized . . . "). To do so is not only unnecessary grammatically but, in the light of the overview of the chapter just given, introduces a thought extraneous to the context. Paul's point is not the incorporating activity of the Spirit at baptism but the necessary share in the one Spirit of all in the body. The Spirit is in view here not as the creator of the body but as the gift granted to all by virtue of their being in the body. The latter is also clearly the point of verse 13b, best understood as reinforcing 13a: "we were all made to drink of one Spirit." The thought is close to Romans 8:9—to belong to Christ is to have the Spirit—and I Corinthians 6:17—to be joined to the Lord is to be one Spirit with him.

Within the context, then, verse 13 focuses on the one (unity) side of the unity-diversity polarity. It may be discussed here in terms of two basic questions:

a. Who is it that has been baptized with the Spirit? Paul's answer is not only plain but emphatic: "we all." "All," of course, does not have an indiscriminately universal reference; it is the all of the one body, the church. Apart from this qualification, however, it may not be further restricted. Paul could not state more clearly that, not just a particular group, some sector within the church, but the entire body, the whole church, has been baptized with the Spirit. The repetition of "all" in verse 13b further accents the universality on his mind at this point. Also, what he goes on to say in the immediately following verses about the spiritual function of every member, no matter how apparently insignificant and dispensable (vv. 22–24), is without foundation, if verse 13 applies only to a part of the body.

b. When were all baptized with the Spirit? At a first glance the verse may not seem to address this question. But the answer is provided by the preposition into (εἰς). The experience of Holy Spirit baptism takes place for each member at the time of incorporation into the one body, at the time of saving inclusion within the covenant community, and not at some time subsequent to that saving incorporation.

To amplify this point briefly, for Paul the basic and, at the same time, all-comprehensive reality of the application of redemption, the alpha and omega of our experience of salvation, is the *experience* of being united to Christ, the life-giving Spirit, and, what is inseparably correlative, being incorporated into his body, the church. This experiential union (incorporation) brings with it the forgiveness of sins (and the imputed righteousness of Christ) and the renewal of life, deliverance from both the guilt and corruption of sin, as well as the continuing enjoyment of these and all other saving benefits.

As Paul also puts the matter, union with Christ (incorporation) means we share in and benefit from what took place once for all in the work of Christ. Stated in this framework, the point of verse 13a is that the experience of being united to Christ (being incorporated into his body) involves an experiential share in the gift of the Spirit with which he baptized the church at Pentecost—just as that union involves an experiential share in his death, resurrection, and ascension (see especially Rom. 6:3f.; Gal. 2:20; Eph. 2:5f.; Col. 2:12f.; 3:1–3), with which, as we have seen (Acts 2:32f.), Pentecost is so indissolubly connected. Holy Spirit baptism, like every other aspect of Christ's once-for-all work, is experienced by the individual believer at the point of incorporation into the church, his Spirit-baptized body.

The emphasis in the preceding two paragraphs on the *experiential* facet of the union in view in verse 13 does not divorce it from nor deny the union of the church with Christ as well both in the eternal design of redemption (Eph. 1:4) and its once-for-all historical accomplishment (see the string of verses already cited in the preceding paragraph). The former (experiential union), however, must be clearly distinguished from the latter two (sometimes this is overlooked).

This understanding of verse 13a points to the sense of the synonymously parallel construction at the end of the verse: those baptized with the Spirit, those who are members of the one body on which the one Spirit has been poured out, are those (emphasizing now the aspect of their reception) who have been made to drink of the one Spirit. The view sometimes set forth that verse 13a refers to Christian (water) baptism, 13b to the Lord's Supper, is not convincing, among other reasons, because it is difficult to see how the practice of recurring observance of the latter can be described by the aorist tense, "were made to drink." Verse 13a, however, does allude to water baptism, inasmuch as the latter signifies and seals union with Christ and all the benefits of that union, including Holy Spirit baptism (the gift of the Spirit). Verse 13, then, plainly teaches (1) that all believers share in the gift of the Spirit and (2) that they do so from the time of their incorporation into the body of Christ. This verse is the hard rock which shatters all constructions of Holy Spirit baptism as an additional, postconversion, second-blessing experience. The outworking of such constructions, in most cases no doubt unintentional but nonetheless inevitable, is stratification within the church between the "haves" and the "have nots," between first and second class citizenship in the kingdom of God, between those alleged to have received the baptism of the Spirit and so to be able to witness effectively and lead a consistent Christian life, and those who are urged to seek Holy Spirit baptism and in the meantime are made to feel miserable because they are led to believe they haven't yet experienced the power of the Spirit. "Second blessing" theologies undermine one of Paul's deepest concerns in chapter 12, namely, that in view of the *spiritual* equality of every part of the body, "there should be no division in the body, but that its parts should have equal concern for each other" (v. 25, NIV). An "un-Spirit-baptized Christian" is a contradiction in terms (cf. Rom. 8:9). The whole church ("all"), not just part of it, is the Pentecostal church. On the individual level, conversion is, among other things, a Pentecost experience.

Finally, even if it should prove that the reference to the Spirit in verse 13a is instrumental ("by one Spirit"), pointing to the Spirit's work of creating the body, verse 13b would still support our basic conclusion from the verse: all believers without exception and by virtue of incorporation into Christ's body share in the gift of the Spirit, the thirst-quenching drink of the Pentecostal waters poured out on the church (see especially John 7:37–39).

This is a good place to comment briefly on Acts 2:38, which should be understood along the same lines as I Corinthians 12:13. Union with (incorporation into the body of) Christ is described here in terms of its basic benefits: remission of sins (justification) and the gift of the Spirit (new life), appropriated by repentance (faith) and sealed by (water) baptism. It is important, then, to recognize that the perspective in verse 38 is different from that in verses 1–13. The latter are concerned with the giving of the Spirit as part of the once-for-all accomplishment of redemption (*historia salutis*), the former with the gift of the Spirit as part of the ongoing, individual application of redemption (*ordo salutis*). The failure to appreciate this difference, as often happens, can be a source of much confusion about the Spirit's work.

4. By now it should be clear that stressing the once-for-all, redemptive-historical character of Pentecost does not have the effect of placing the events of Acts in the remote past, as historical curiosities with little or no bearing on the present experience of believers. On the contrary, to point up the integral place of Pentecost in the once-for-all work of Christ is to do the same for the gift of the Spirit in the experience of everyone united to Christ. The Spirit, poured out on the church and present in and through its Head, is the power given to all, not only some, believers, and intended to redirect lives and leave no aspect of our experience untransformed.

Here I limit myself to expanding our discussion in two directions.

a. To maintain that all believers have been baptized with the Spirit is not to exclude subsequent growth and individual variations in each believer's experience of the Spirit's work, nor to deny that subsequently some may have an experience (or experiences) of the Spirit's transforming power which may make a more memorable impact than conversion. The Spirit's ongoing activity in its individual variations is described in the New Testament as the "filling" or "fulness" of the Spirit. Ephesians 5:18, the only place in the New Testament where believers are commanded to be filled with the Spirit, is most instructive here. The form of the imperative (present tense), as often pointed out, accents that what is commanded is to be done continuously or repeatedly, not just once. This, by the way, is an indication that the filling of the Spirit is not identical with the baptism of the Spirit. Unlike the latter in its once-for-all occurrence at conversion, being filled with the Spirit is an ongoing process or activity in the Christian life. The

command of verse 18 may be variously paraphrased: "be continually full of the Spirit," "be filled with the Spirit again and again,"
"constantly be seeking a fuller outworking of the Spirit in your
life." This command, it should be stressed, is relevant to all believers throughout the whole of their lives. No believer may pre-
sume to have experienced a definitive filling of the Spirit so that
the command of verse 18 no longer applies. Short of death or the
Lord's return, it continues in effect for every believer. One mark of
truly Spirit-filled Christians is that they are not preoccupied with
some working of the Spirit in their past, but are concerned with
what the Spirit is presently doing in their lives and with even
greater workings (fillings) there may be in the future.

How are believers to obey this command to be filled with the
Spirit? Without trying here to give a thorough answer, two considerations may be pointed out.

(1) The participial clauses that make up verses 19–21 are dependent syntactically on the command of verse 18 and modify its
subject. These verses, then, are best taken as explaining the filling
work of the Spirit. They describe several of its inevitable results,
things we should expect to find in those filled with the Spirit.
Obviously Paul is not trying to be exhaustive here, but surely he
mentions what is most prominent and of greatest concern for him.
Further, 5:22—6:9 is plainly structured around the theme of
mutual subjection picked up from verse 21 and so is fairly taken as
explaining the filling work of the Spirit in marriage (5:22–33), in
the family (6:1–4), and on the job (6:5–9). Being filled with the
Spirit means marriages that work and are not poisoned by suspi-
cion and bitterness; homes where parents, children, brothers and
sisters really enjoy being with each other, free from jealousy and
resentment; and job situations that are not oppressive and depersonalizing, but meaningful and truly rewarding.

(2) In the close parallel of Ephesians 5:18—6:9 to Colossians
3:16—4:1, probably reflecting some overall genetic tie between
the two letters, the command to be filled with the Spirit is re-
placed by "Let the word of Christ dwell in you richly." In view of
the parallelism involved we are bound to conclude that the filling
of the Spirit and the richly indwelling Word of Christ are
functionally equivalent. That indwelling Word is not some

specialized or restricted truth granted only to some in the congregation but "everything I have commanded you" (Matt. 28:20),
faithfully believed and obeyed.

The filling of the Spirit, then, is not a matter of unusual or
spectacular experience (although something of that may at times
be involved) but Spirit-worked obedience to Christ as that comes
to expression in the basic, everyday relationships and respon-
sibilities of life. The reality of the Spirit's filling work is the reality, in all its breadth and richness, of the ongoing working of
Christ, the life-giving Spirit, with his Word. To look for some
word other than this Word, now inscripturated for the church,
is to be seeking some spirit other than the Holy Spirit. All told,
to be filled with the Spirit is "to be strengthened with power
through His Spirit in the inner man; so that Christ may dwell in
your hearts through faith; that you, being rooted and grounded in
love, . . . may be filled up to all the fulness of God" (Eph. 3:16, 17,
19, NASB).

b. I Corinthians 3:1–3 ought not to be seen as rationalizing or
regularizing the existence within the church of two classes of
Christians, carnal and spiritual. Although this may be the initial
impression the passage leaves, reading it in this way effectively
undercuts Paul's basic point. For one thing, these verses will have
to be understood in the light of what Paul has just said at the close
of chapter 2. There he draws as sharply as anywhere in his letters
the absolute cleavage that runs through mankind (vv. 14f.). All
people are in one of two classes; there are "natural" men (i.e.,
those without the Spirit) and spiritual men, and no middle ground
between them. It would not only be highly unlikely but contradictory, then, for Paul to go on in effect to introduce yet another,
third class of people in 3:1ff. Moreover, the adjectives used in
these verses and usually translated "carnal," "fleshy," "worldly"
(σάρκινος, σαρκικός), against the background of Paul's use of the
antithesis between Spirit and "flesh" (cf. especially Rom. 8:4ff.;
Gal. 5:16ff.), are plainly synonymous with "natural" (ψυχικός) in
2:14, indicating what is devoid of the Spirit and in opposition to
his working.

Paul's indictment in 3:1ff., then, is not that the Corinthians are
behaving like low-level, second-class Christians, but that they are

not behaving like Christians *at all*, that their behavior is in *contradiction* to their identity and confession as believers. Paul must impress on his readers that there is no greater or more distressing anomaly than the divisions existing in their midst. This is confirmed in verse 3 by Paul's specification of their sin as "jealousy and strife," a combination occurring elsewhere in Paul in Galatians 5:20, where it is among the deeds of the "flesh" standing in unrelieved opposition to the Spirit and his fruits, and in Romans 13:13 as deeds of darkness in conflict with the light (cf. II Cor. 12:20).

Nor should it be thought that "infants in Christ" (v. 1) supports some form of the carnal-spiritual stratification argued against here. This expression has its sense in the light of Paul's description of Christians in 2:6 as "perfect" or "mature." This maturity is not a Christian attainment demonstrated only by some, but the possession of the *whole* congregation *in Christ* (cf. 1:24, 30). It is the *normal* state of *all* believers, with which each *begins* the Christian life. Accordingly, "infants in Christ" is not meant to soften Paul's otherwise harsh words by conceding the mitigating circumstance of their being young Christians, new in the faith. Rather, it reveals the thoroughly abnormal, regressive state of affairs at Corinth. "Puerile," "infantile," "retarded" capture Paul's nuance (cf. Heb. 5:12f.). To be sure, he does address them as Christians (v. 1), but his point is that everything about their divisive behavior is incompatible with that identity and tends towards its destruction.

5. Efforts are frequently made to identify the significance of Pentecost in terms of differences between the experience of new covenant and old covenant believers. This brings into view a large question, in need of much more thorough discussion than the brief remarks made here. These attempt only to express guidelines essential for an overall understanding of the complex issues involved.

a. After surveying at length the heroic and exemplary faith of old covenant believers, the writer of Hebrews concludes: "Yet none of them received what had been promised. God had planned something better for us so that only together with us would they be made perfect" (Heb. 11:39f., NIV). What does this "something better" of the new covenant (cf. 7:22; 8:6) entail for the experience of those presently under its gracious administration? Taken as a whole the New Testament indicates one clear and fundamental difference between the experience of old and new covenant believers. That is the (spiritual) union New Testament believers have with Christ, the life-giving Spirit, and so, in Christ, with each other (in the church, his body). This union, as union with the *exalted* Christ, is the immediate ground and source of all the other blessings of salvation, yet it was not enjoyed prior to Christ's death and resurrection. Old Testament believers were regenerated, justified, and sanctified on the basis of Christ's (future) work, but the mode of covenant fellowship in which they experienced these blessings was provisional and lacked the finality and permanence of union with (the glorified) Christ.

The momentous, unprecedented reality of this union can hardly be overemphasized. It involves a relationship to the covenanting God that is nothing less than eschatological in its intimacy and perfections. It is central to those kingdom blessings finally revealed in Christ, which "many prophets and righteous men" longed to experience but did not (Matt. 13:16f.). It includes the reception of adoption as sons and of the Spirit as the Spirit of adoption, in contrast to the slave/minor condition of old covenant believers (Rom. 8:14–17; Gal. 3:23—4:7). It fulfills the promise of a "new heart of flesh," of the indwelling Spirit, and of the writing of God's law on the heart (Ezek. 36:26f.; Jer. 31:33).

b. But what further, *in detail*, are the experiential implications of the difference this union creates? Here Scripture is elusive. A concern to identify and stress the newness of the Spirit's work under the new covenant must not lead us to eclipse or perhaps even deny the reality of his activity in believers under the old covenant. Admittedly, explicit Old Testament references to the Spirit's work in individuals are sparse, but to structure the difference between old and new by the disjunction between theocratic endowment and personal indwelling (the Spirit "on" and "in") is not only unconvincing but wrong. For example, both factors interweave, in my judgment, with the accent on the latter, in David's prayer: "Do not take your Holy Spirit from me" (Ps. 51:11). In a context that reflects an intense concern about sin, repentance, forgiveness, and salvation, a concern which obviously flows from the deepest recesses of his person, surely more is at stake in David's plea than the loss of his theocratic prerogatives and powers.

The response that such a prayer is not appropriate for a New Testament believer, who has received the gift of the Spirit, does not take into account the urgent, almost ominous tone in which the writer of Hebrews warns and exhorts the church against apostasy (e.g., 3:12f.; 4:1), as well as the linking of the experience of the old covenant community and the New Testament church by the common thought of grieving the Spirit (cf. Eph. 4:30 with Isa. 63:10). Further and more substantially, vast stretches of Old Testament experience, for example, the (representative) faith of Abraham and the piety and prayers of the Psalms, are only to be explained as expressions of what the New Testament clearly teaches is the Spirit's sovereign work of inner renewal and personal transformation. This may not have been the average experience in Israel, but it was still the model and is essentially continuous with that of the New Testament. Can we say that New Testament believers are capable of more sublime praise of God, deeper devotion to him, and greater fervency in prayer than, say, we find expressed in the Psalms of David and others? (This reference to the Psalms ought not to be undercut by appealing to their unique, inspired origin. They are at the same time the heartfelt conviction of their writers, to be shared and voiced by all in Israel.) Can we say more here than that in view of the fulfillment realized in Christ we are able to read (and sing) the Psalms with deeper insight and appreciation than old covenant believers could?

c. This last question hints at the direction our thinking should take. We must recognize that Scripture is just not interested in the question of individual religious experience in the way we are inclined to be preoccupied with it. What the New Testament does disclose of the individual repercussions of the Spirit's work largely results as it accents the broader christological and ecclesiological concerns already discussed. Along these lines the difference between old and new covenants is clear.

(1) Christ has become life-giving Spirit. The Spirit is now present as a result of the actually finished work of Christ; he is present not, as previously under the old covenant, proleptically, "ahead of time," in terms of promise, but properly present "in due season," on the basis of the actual fulfillment, apart from which the promise is ultimately null and void. This is the sense of John 7:39: "The Spirit had not yet been given, because Jesus was not yet glorified." On the one side, this statement should not be toned down to say in effect that the Spirit is now more fully present, present to a greater degree, than under the old covenant; it expresses absolutely what formerly was not and now is the case. On the other hand, it should not be so abstractly absolutized that it conflicts with the undeniable indications of the Spirit's activity in the Old Testament. Recognition of its redemptive-historical, christological thrust maintains the required balance.

(2) The Spirit now present is the *universal* Spirit; the Spirit is present in the new covenant community, now no longer restricted to Israel, now expanded to include both Israel and the nations, Gentiles as well as Jews. In contrast to the old covenant the Spirit is now poured out on all "flesh" (Acts 2:17). The Spirit is the "blessing of Abraham" come to the Gentiles (Gal. 3:14), the Spirit of the kingdom taken away from the old Israel and given to a nation (the new Israel) producing its fruits (Matt. 21:43). This unprecedented worldwide dominion of the Spirit (Christ, the life-giving Spirit) is a function of Pentecost. The Spirit of Pentecost is the Spirit of mission.

These two accents constitute the major emphasis of the New Testament on the differences in the Spirit's activity between old and new covenants. That experiential implications are involved is no doubt true and some are plain, for example, union with Christ and the privilege, power, and responsibility New Testament believers have for worldwide gospel witness. But for the most part they stand in the background and come into view only obliquely so that spelling them out will probably always contain an element of the problematic.

Perhaps the larger lesson to learn here is that while individual experience is precious and indispensable to being a Christian, it is not to be our primary concern. That concern is the coming of the kingdom of God, the eschatological lordship of Christ over all creation established in "the fulness of time" (Gal. 4:4), particularly by his death, resurrection, ascension, and Pentecost. Here too we may rest content that the words of Jesus in

Matthew 6:33 apply: Seek first the kingdom of God and his righteousness and all these things, experience included, will be given
to you as well.

Note on John 20:22

"He breathed on them and said, 'Receive the Holy Spirit.'"
This statement is one of the perennial cruxes of New Testament
interpretation, particularly its relationship to Acts 2. The problem
is that in Acts the Spirit comes on Pentecost, fifty days after the
resurrection, while here the Spirit is given on the day of the resurrection itself. The consensus of modern historical-critical interpretation is that this is the "Johannine Pentecost" and a classic example of contradiction within the New Testament, in this case
conflict between the theology of John and the theology of Luke-
Acts. Before considering some solutions to this difficulty, several
factors bearing on it may be noted.

1. In any approach the *differences* between the two passages
need to be kept in view. Despite apparently similar references to
the Holy Spirit, these differences are multiple and pronounced.
Not only is there the difference in time already noted, but in each
instance the overall conditions are dissimilar: John—a secret, at
least restricted gathering at evening (cf. v. 19); Acts—the middle
of the morning with immediate public consequences. The recipients in John are the closest circle of disciples with even Thomas
absent; in Acts, the entire Jerusalem congregation ("all," 2:1; cf.
1:15). In John, Jesus is present bodily; in Acts, he is not present
bodily. All these considerations point to the fact that we are deal-
ing with something other than varying or contradictory accounts
of the same event. Rather, we are faced with accounts of two
different events, accounts requiring to be related.

2. John records much more fully than the Synoptics Jesus' own
promise of the Spirit's coming (especially chaps. 14-16). At
14:12ff. the giving of the Spirit as Paraclete (v. 16) is connected
with the fact that Jesus is about to go to the Father (that is, the
ascension, v. 12). This tie is made most explicit in 16:7: "It is to
your advantage that I go away. For unless I go away, the Paraclete

will not come to you; but if I go, I will send him to you." The
sending of the promised Spirit follows and is contingent on the
ascension. But in 20:22 Jesus is clearly presented as not yet ascended. (See his response to Mary, v. 17: "I have not yet ascended
to the Father.") So to view 20:22 as the Johannine Pentecost brings
John into conflict not only with Luke but himself, his own theological structure.

3. We can recall here our discussion (pp. 27f.) of Luke 24:53.
Luke suggests a transforming experience of some kind for the disciples after the resurrection and before Pentecost (cf. vv. 32, 45),
an experience resulting in open praise (positive witness).

Conclusion: Why Luke makes no mention of the event of John
20:22 is difficult to say. Still, what is the relationship of that event
to Pentecost? That relationship is perhaps best understood in
terms of the "staging" principle that marks the coming of the
kingdom of God. Just as at the time of Jesus' public ministry the
one, eschatological kingdom both had come (Matt. 12:28) and was
also "at hand" (Matt. 4:17), both in the immediate future of the
resurrection, ascension, and Pentecost (Matt. 16:28) as well as the
more distant return of Christ (Matt. 25:31, 34), so too the one, eschatological kingdom-gift of the Spirit is given both on the day of
the resurrection and Pentecost. The former is a kind of firstfruits of
the latter, Pentecost itself being the day of firstfruits (Num. 28:26)
of the full harvest of the Spirit to come at Christ's return (Rom.
8:23). The event of John 20:22, then, is the "firstfruits of the firstfruits." A tie with Pentecost is also suggested by verse 23, almost
identical to the "power of the keys" statement in Matthew 16:19
which is tied there to Jesus' promise to build the church (v. 18),
a promise fulfilled at Pentecost.

The event of John 20:22 also shows Jesus to be the giver of the
Spirit (life) or "life-giving Spirit" (Paul) by virtue of his resurrection, and so provides the dynamic for the praise activity of Luke
24:53. In this connection, some have plausibly suggested that the
verb "he breathed" (ἐνεφύσησεν), which occurs only here in the
New Testament, is an echo of Genesis 2:7, where in the Septuagint
(the Greek translation of the Old Testament) it describes God's
activity in creating man. As the preincarnate Word was active in
creation and the source of life from the beginning (John 1:3f.), so

now the resurrected Christ is the beginning and source of the new creation. (Cf. also the use of this verb to describe God's breathing activity of enlivening—Ezek. 37:9; cf. I Kings 17:21—and destroying—Job 41:21; Ezek. 21:31; 22:21, in the latter two instances associated with the fire of wrath. Both activities are intimated in the prophecy of John the Baptist [Luke 3:16f.], fulfilled at Pentecost.)

This understanding of John 20:22, whatever difficulties still remain, seems preferable to other proposed solutions. The view that John describes the gift of the Spirit to the apostles as the foundation of the church, while Acts describes the gift of the Spirit to the entire church, has against it that the apostles were waiting with the rest of the church for Pentecost (Acts 1:4; cf. Luke 24:49) and were apparently fully involved recipients. Also, can we be sure that only the ten (minus Thomas) were present in John 20:22? The view that John records a purely symbolic action of Jesus, prophetic of Pentecost, has surface plausibility. But it is difficult to resist the notion that an actual communication of the Spirit is involved.

On the assumption the disciples were already regenerate men (John 6:68f.) and John 20:22 describes a different event than does Acts 2, the difficulty of this passage for "second blessing" doctrines is apparent. The point again is that this event is not part of a model to be repeated in the experience of believers in every generation, but was an aspect of the unique experience of those who lived at the time of the cross and resurrection, and made up the first, foundational generation of the church.

III

Some Basic Perspectives on the Gifts of the Spirit

The passages that figure most prominently in the discussion of what are usually termed "spiritual" or "charismatic" gifts are Romans 12:3–8, I Corinthians 12–14, and Ephesians 4:7–13. This chapter introduces a number of general considerations necessary for gaining a proper understanding of these and related passages as well as the particular gifts mentioned in them.

A. The Gift of the Spirit and the Gifts of the Spirit

The distinction between the gift and the gifts of the Spirit functions in two interrelated senses.

1. The work of the Spirit (the gift) experienced by *all* in the church, the Spirit given on the principle of "universal donation," is to be distinguished from those workings of the Spirit (the gifts) *variously distributed* within the church, the Spirit given on the principle of "differential distribution." Both these principles are clearly expressed in I Corinthians 12, the former in verse 13 (universal donation: all baptized with, all made to drink of, the one

Spirit), the latter in verses 29, 30 (differential distribution: all are not apostles, all are not prophets, etc.).

2. The gift (singular) of the Spirit is integral to the experience of salvation in Christ (repentance unto life, Acts 11:18). It is an actual foretaste of eschatological life, the anticipatory "firstfruits" of the future resurrection harvest (Rom. 8:23), the "down payment" in kind on the final inheritance (II Cor. 1:22; 5:5; Eph. 1:13f.). On the other hand, the gifts (plural) of the Spirit consist of particular operations pertaining to various ministries (I Cor. 12:4-6) and, as such, are provisional and subeschatological. This is one of Paul's points in I Corinthians 13:8ff., a passage touched on here only briefly because we will be returning to it below. Prophecy and tongues, among other gifts, have a provisional and partial character and so are temporary, destined to pass away (vv. 8f.), while those works of the Spirit like faith, hope, and love endure (v. 13).

It is necessary, then, in considering the whole work of the one Spirit in the church, to recognize on the one hand those activities and outworkings that are eschatological and experienced by all, and on the other hand those subeschatological functions, none of which is given to all. It is essential to distinguish what is present eschatologically by universal donation from what is given subeschatologically by differential distribution.

The reader ought to be fully aware of the fundamental control exerted by this distinction. The subsequent course of the entire discussion is decisively determined by it. Involved is a rejection of all constructions that find the essence of the new covenant (the eschatological order already present) to be in or inevitably associated with a particular gift or combination of gifts or even the sum total of gifts, a rejection of all constructions that define (at least partially) the newness of the new covenant in terms of those gifts. For one thing, confining our attention to biblical history, we note that certain gifts or at least the distinctive phenomena associated with them are not unique to the new covenant but are also found under the old covenant. Prophecy and healing certainly, and perhaps something at least very similar to, if not identical with, tongues (I Sam. 10:7, 10-13; 19:23f.), serve as examples.

Also, something more should be said here about the provisional nature of gifts in a new covenant context. This can be done by reflecting briefly on the significance of the healing miracles of Jesus and the apostles.

Something like a middle-road approach to these miracles seems called for. Performed in the context of the arrival of the final kingdom (Luke 11:20; cf., e.g., Acts 1:3; 8:12; 20:25), they are nevertheless not of its essence. The latter point needs further explanation. Certainly these miracles are not merely external signs which more or less arbitrarily point away from themselves to purely invisible, transcendent, or inward realities (like justification and regeneration). They are not simply external parables of inward realities. Rather they appropriately and necessarily disclose the essence of the kingdom and its blessings, but without at the same time constituting or embodying that essence.

An instructive example is the resurrection of Lazarus (John 11). This event doesn't simply point away to regeneration or inner renewal and cleansing from sin. Rather it shows that Jesus' claim in the Gospel ("I am the resurrection and the life," v. 25) has to do with the *whole* man, that salvation in Christ concerns the restoration of sinners in their psychosomatic wholeness, body as well as soul. Lazarus' resurrection points to the glorified, spiritual resurrection to be received by believers at Christ's return. But—and this is the point—through the miracle Lazarus does not receive that glorified body; eventually he dies, is buried, and with other dead believers awaits the resurrection. The same observations apply, for example, to the raising of Dorcas by Peter (Acts 9:36–42), and of Eutychus by Paul (Acts 20:9–12). In this sense, then, the variously distributed workings of the Spirit, of which the healings of Jesus and the apostles are an instance, are provisional and, in some instances, function as signs. Accordingly, each gift has to be examined in order to determine its specific purpose(s) and the specific conditions for its presence in the church.

The purpose of these remarks is not to depreciate spiritual gifts or promote a cavalier treatment of them, but to set them in a balanced perspective. To sum up again: the gift of the Spirit, shared by all believers, is the eschatological essence of the new covenant, the fulfillment of the Father's promise, the down payment and firstfruits of resurrected life. The gifts of the Spirit, while particular expressions of this life, are *provisional* expressions. Necessitated by, bound up with, and shaped by the conditions that make up "the form of this world [which] is passing away" (I Cor. 7:31), they are themselves transient (the point of I Cor. 13:8–10). The balance intended here may be difficult to grasp and maintain, but it is crucial.

B. Charismatic and Noncharismatic

To refer to the gifts and activities listed in Romans 12, I Corinthians 12, and Ephesians 4 as charismatic in order to distinguish them from presumably noncharismatic gifts and functions in the church is at best misleading. One way this can be seen is by surveying the use of the key term χάρισμα, from which "charisma" and "charismatic" come. The word is used distinctively, almost exclusively, by Paul. This generalization includes not only the other New Testament writers but the extrabiblical Greek literature contemporary with them. Paul is apparently the first to make it an important (theological) term. This makes its relatively wide range of meaning all the more significant.

In Romans 12:6 and I Corinthians 12:4ff., its best known usage, the word describes a variety of specific gifts present in the context of the congregation and intended to function for its edification. But "spiritual gift" in Romans 1:11 (the only place where this adjective and noun are used together: "I long to see you so that I may impart to you some spiritual gift to make you strong," NIV) most likely does not have in view one of the gifts listed in Romans 12 or I Corinthians 12, but the overall strengthening Paul desires his presence and ministry to be among the Roman Christians, "that you and I may be mutually encouraged by each other's faith" (v. 12). The usage in I Corinthians 1:7 most likely has a similar general sense. In II Corinthians 1:11 ("the gracious favor granted us") the word refers to a specific event, Paul's deliverance from a particularly perilous situation (cf. v. 10), while according to I Corinthians 7:7 ("each man has his own gift from God") either marriage or celibacy can be a *charisma*. I Timothy 4:14 and II

Timothy 1:6 use the term to refer to the capacity granted to Timothy by the laying on of hands for the faithful exercise of his ministerial office. The plural usage in Romans 11:29 ("the gifts and calling of God are irrevocable") has in view the various covenant privileges of Israel (cf. 3:1, 2; 9:4). The more general force of the word is particularly noteworthy in Romans 5:15, 16:

> But the gift [χάρισμα] is not like the trespass. For if the many died by the trespass of the one man, how much more did God's grace [χάρις] and the gift that came by the grace [ἡ δωρεὰ ἐν χάριτι] of the one man, Jesus Christ, overflow to many. Again, the gift [δώρημα] of God is not like the result of the one man's sin: The judgment followed one sin and brought condemnation, but the gift [χάρισμα] followed many trespasses and brought justification. (NIV)

In the deliberately developed parallelism of these verses, χάρισμα is used interchangeably with other words for "gift" and overlaps in meaning with χάρις ("grace"). It refers quite sweepingly to the righteousness and life graciously revealed in Christ (cf. vv. 17, 20). Similarly, in Romans 6:23 the χάρισμα of God is, quite comprehensively, "eternal life."

To sum up, "gift" (χάρισμα) is a flexible term, used in various senses. These, however, are not unrelated. The consideration that apparently underlies and unifies them, giving rise to the flexibility noted, is this: every gift (χάρισμα) is a manifestation of grace (χάρις), and any manifestation of grace can be termed a gift. Paul himself says as much in Romans 12:6: "We have different gifts, according to the grace given us."

Both in its origin and continuation the church exists solely by God's grace. The *whole* church, then, in *all* its aspects and activities is properly seen as charismatic. From an individual angle, the life of faith is such by grace (Eph. 2:8) and so in its entirety, from beginning to end, charismatic. Accordingly, to identify certain gifts in the church as charismatic in order to distinguish them in this way from others runs the risk of distorting or narrowing Paul's perspective. And when, as too often happens, "charismatic" in this restricted sense becomes virtually equated with gifts, or the "real" gifts (the "ones that really count"), then the result is nothing less than impoverishing.

Similarly, the way the distinction between the gifts and fruits of the Spirit is sometimes made betrays a schematization foreign to Paul, if the fruits are not seen as gifts. No doubt certain workings of the Spirit are intended for and in fact given to only some in the church (I Cor. 12:29f.), while the fruits of the Spirit are intended for and ought to be present in all (Gal. 5:22ff.). But the latter, no less than the former, are gifts of the Spirit.

Certainly some gifts involve distinctive endowment beyond the normal capacities of the recipient (e.g., prophecy and tongues, as we shall see below). But the direction of Paul's teaching is fairly expressed as follows: any capacity of the believer, including aptitudes present before conversion, brought under the controlling power of God's grace and functioning in his service is a spiritual gift. Spiritual gifts comprise *all* the ways in which God by the power of his Spirit uses Christians as instruments in his service. I Corinthians 7:7 is an instructive example of this breadth: celibacy or marriage, as the case may be, ought to be and can be a spiritual ministry. Biblically speaking, "charismatic" and "Christian" are synonymous. The Christian life in its totality is (to be) a charismatic life. Christ's church as a *whole* is *the* charismatic movement.

C. The Trinitarian Character of the Gifts

1. To refer to the gifts listed in Romans 12, I Corinthians 12, and Ephesians 4 as spiritual is only partly correct and may miss the larger picture. Because of the functional unity between the Spirit and Christ, dating from the exaltation of the latter (I Cor. 15:45), their work is inseparable. Accordingly, in Ephesians 4:7ff. the ascended Christ gives gifts. Further, the Spirit in all his activities is "the promise of the Father" (Luke 24:49; Acts 1:4; cf. 2:33), so that the more general references to God as the giver of gifts (Rom. 12:3; I Cor. 12:28), in keeping with Paul's customary usage, refer implicitly to the Father. At any rate, I Corinthians 12:4–6 (cf. Eph. 4:4–6) provides an expressly trinitarian, fully theological

perspective on the bestowal of gifts. The gifts are not only the Spirit's, but Christ's and the Father's, and this breadth in outlook is necessary for correcting a by no means imaginary tendency to one-sided emphasis on the Spirit in the matter of gifts in the church.

2. Still, it would be wrong to overlook the accent on the Spirit, particularly in I Corinthians 12–14. The giving of gifts is "the manifestation of the Spirit" (12:7; cf. vv. 8f.). The Spirit "distributes to each one as he wills" (12:11). The use of the adjective *spiritual* (πνευματικός) in this context is instructive. Some maintain that it is not so much Paul's own choice as a matter of accommodation on his part to the preference and specialized usage of some among his Corinthian readers. But it is difficult to disprove that in 14:1 (cf. 12:1) Paul has made its usage as a plural noun a virtual synonym for "gifts." Also the expression "spiritual gift" (Rom. 1:11) shows how closely he associates the Spirit with gifts given to the church and how natural and appropriate he finds it to describe them in terms of the Spirit's work. (His point is hardly to distinguish some gifts from others not of the Spirit; cf. the remarks on this verse above under point B.)

D. The Ministerial Character of the Gifts

From beginning to end gifts are given for *service* in the church. There are no exceptions to this consideration. The ministerial purpose of gifts is especially plain in I Corinthians 12:4ff. In the most likely understanding of verses 4–6 with their triadic structure, "gifts" (v. 4), "ministries" (v. 5) and "workings" (v. 6) do not refer to different entities but define each other so that the latter two serve to identify the nature of the former, and to make plain that the gifts listed in the following verses (8–10) are to function for service within the church. The diverse, multifaceted manifestation of the Spirit is "for the common good" (v. 7). And the consideration that identifies the purpose of all gifts and regulates their exercise is the edification of the church (I Cor. 14:12; cf. v. 26: "all things . . . for edification").

The ministerial nature of *all* gifts carries the implication that the beneficial subjective, emotional response the exercise of a particular gift may bring to its recipient is always an aspect of that gift (given for ministry), not an additional, separable gift. Consequently, such experiences are not independent of the principle of edification already noted but are strictly ancillary to it. They are "fringe benefits."

E. Holy Spirit Baptism and the Gifts

The view that a particular gift (e.g., tongues) is the (almost) invariable accompaniment that serves to evidence Spirit baptism as a distinct, (usually) postconversion experience finds no real support in the New Testament and in fact runs counter to its teaching on the baptism (gift) of the Holy Spirit (cf. above, pp. 22–32). No gift can claim a "privileged" position or have its place in the life of the church maintained as a component in a "second blessing" or Spirit-baptism theology. The continuing place of each gift must be established by considering it in its own right in order to determine its distinctive character and intended function. And that will always be, in one way or another, as just noted, for the edification of the church.

F. Gifts and Office

Both in the exegetical and dogmatic discussions of the past seventy-five to one hundred years, few questions have been so intensely and widely debated as the question of the relationship between gift and office. This is so because the question has been at the center of the struggle between competing, sometimes mutually exclusive conceptions of the nature of the earliest ("primitive") Christianity. I touch on this relationship here only to indicate the distance between the New Testament itself and the different variations of a viewpoint that has proved very influential, especially within the "historical-critical" tradition of biblical interpretation, but recently has asserted itself more widely. At the same time this will further set the tone of our own discussion.

Any tension or opposition between gift (the Spirit) and office is totally foreign to the New Testament. Any construction by which the Spirit as a principle of unstructured freedom and unformed spontaneity is set in conflict with considerations of established order and stable structure is not based on New Testament teaching but in most instances reflects the alien problematics of post-Enlightenment, post-Kantian ontology and epistemology (even where the Enlightenment and Kant may never have been heard of!).

The harmony present in the outlook of the New Testament is clear from the "official" use of χάρισμα in the Pastoral Epistles (I Tim. 4:14: " . . . the gift, given you through prophecy with the laying on of hands by the presbytery"; cf. II Tim. 1:6; Titus 1:5: " . . . that you might set in order what remains, and appoint elders in every city as I directed you," NASB). There is also the unmistakable office character of the apostolate. The positive integration that should exist between gifts and office raises important and quite practical issues for the life of the congregation. These deserve a study of their own. Here I have tried only to point out the controlling point of departure for such a study. The one and same Spirit is the Spirit of both ardor and order.

G. The Composition of the Lists of Gifts
(Rom. 12:6–8; I Cor. 12:8–10, 28; Eph. 4:11)

These lists, as is frequently pointed out but more often overlooked, are not complete, but selective and representative. However, so far Paul's rationale for selection in each case has not been demonstrated conclusively. Without presuming to do that here, at least two generalizations can be made about the composition of these listings taken as a whole.

1. Too sharp a line should not be drawn between many of the gifts. For example, it is doubtful whether anyone has successfully demonstrated exegetically a clear difference between "the word of wisdom" and "the word of knowledge" (I Cor. 12:8). Similarly, it seems difficult to distinguish sharply between "gifts of healing" and "miraculous powers" (I Cor. 12:9, 10), or between "teaching" and "exhorting" (Rom. 12:7, 8). In the light of the overall teaching of the New Testament, the listing in I Corinthians 12:28 ("first apostles, second prophets, third teachers") seems to involve a kind of hierarchy whereby each of the latter two consists of an aspect of the preceding gift(s), that is, prophecy is a function of the apostle, and teaching, in turn, a function of both the prophet and apostle. Paul, for instance, exercises the predictive function of the prophet (e.g., Rom. 11:25f.; I Cor. 15:51ff.; I Thess. 4:15ff.; II Thess. 2:3ff.) and twice sweepingly identifies himself as a teacher as well as an apostle (I Tim. 2:7; II Tim. 1:11). Acts 13:1 names several individuals, including Paul (Saul), and describes this group as "prophets and teachers," without distinguishing among them. All this suggests a degree of overlap between certain gifts as well as the exercise, in some instances, of more than one by a given individual (e.g., the apostle).

2. The apparently random character of the lists should not keep us from recognizing that each of the gifts belongs to one of two basic categories: *word*-charismata and *deed*-charismata. These two are of course inseparable and closely supplement each other in the life of the church. At the same time, the distinction between verbal and nonverbal activity ought not to be overlooked or minimized. Any particular gift is either a service in word or a service in deed, with several, notably apostleship, involving both kinds of ministry.

Confirmation for viewing the various lists of gifts in terms of this basic profile is found in I Peter 4:10, 11 (the only occurrence of χάρισμα outside Paul's letters):

> Each one should use whatever spiritual gift he has received to serve others, faithfully administering God's grace in its various forms. If anyone speaks, he should do it as one speaking the very words of God. If anyone serves, he should do it with the strength God provides. . . . (NIV)

Not inappropriately these verses may be taken as providing a brief, compressed overview of the entire New Testament teaching on spiritual gifts. Notice how a number of the considerations already discussed combine here: the variously distributed character of the gifts given to the congregation, the gifts as particular manifestations of the grace of God, the ministerial nature of the gifts, and the dual profiling of gifts in terms of word and deed.

H. Identifying Your Gift(s)

"How can I discover my gift(s)?" This question is being asked by Christians today with increasing frequency and concern to be involved actively in the life of the church. Beyond what has already been said by way of answer under the preceding points (e.g., the broad scope of spiritual gifts, including even our "natural" capacities and aptitudes, and the ministerial, functional nature of gifts), several matters need to be emphasized here. For one thing, what is best described as an abstract or mechanical approach to the question of gifts ought to be avoided. Such an approach begins with a kind of spiritual self-inventory in the light of the lists in Romans 12, I Corinthians 12, Ephesians 4 and then proceeds to pray for a particular gift desired or felt to be lacking. More than we are perhaps aware, such an attitude may betray more of our contemporary Western mentality with its penchant for the specialist than genuine New Testament spirituality. Further, according to the New Testament this approach is wrong: (1) it is unduly restrictive because, as already noted, the lists are selective and not intended to be complete; and (2) it creates confusion because, as I will try to show below, some of the gifts are temporary by design and do not continue beyond the time of the apostles.

The way to determine our spiritual gifts is not to ask, "What is my 'thing' spiritually, my spiritual specialty, that sets me apart from other believers and gives me a distinguishing niche in the church?" Rather the New Testament on the whole takes a much more *functional* or *situational* approach. The question to ask is, "What in the situation in which God has placed me are the particular opportunities I see for serving other believers in word and deed (cf. I Peter 4:10f.)?" "What are the specific needs confronting me that need to be ministered to?" Posing and effectively responding to this question will go a long way not only toward discovering but also actually using our spiritual gifts.

The final word in this connection stems from the experience of

Paul. Extraordinarily gifted among Christians in the New Testament (e.g., Acts 19:11f.; 28:3-6, 8f.; I Cor. 9:1f.; II Cor. 12:1ff.), nevertheless only as he was brought face to face with his own limitations and weakness, did he come to recognize the true secret of his usefulness in the church (II Cor. 12:7ff.). Granted sublime experiences (vv. 2f.) and indescribable revelations (v. 4), he was also given a "thorn in the flesh" to keep him from exalting himself (v. 7) and to impress him with the power of Christ, efficacious through the medium of his own weakness (v. 9), so that "when I am weak, then I am strong" (v. 10).

Probably the most important and certainly the most difficult lesson for us to learn is that ultimately spiritual gifts are not our presumed strengths and abilities, not something that we "have" (or even have been given), but what God does through us in spite of ourselves and our weakness. "My grace is sufficient for you, for my power is made perfect in weakness" (II Cor. 12:9). This word of the exalted Christ, to us as well as Paul, is the bottom line to the existence of every Christian, including the matter of our spiritual gifts.

IV

Prophecy and Tongues

Present day controversy over spiritual gifts centers predominantly on tongues and prophecy, to a somewhat lesser degree on healing. This development determines the focus on prophecy and tongues in this and the next chapter. In this chapter we will be concerned particularly with the nature or basic characteristics of these gifts. The reason for treating them together, if not already apparent, will become clear presently.

A. I Corinthians 14: Some Controlling Observations

The only place in the New Testament where either prophecy or tongues are dealt with in a sustained, more than passing fashion is I Corinthians 14, set in a context (chaps. 12–14) where Paul devotes attention to the gifts operative in the church at Corinth. While the problems he has in view may have been peculiar to the Corinthian congregation, the gifts discussed are surely those present in the other congregations mentioned in the New Testament (e.g., Jerusalem, Antioch, Ephesus, Rome). In this respect, the situation at Corinth can be seen as typical of others in the New Testament.

Several considerations are on the surface of chapter 14 and set the direction for further discussion of the gifts mentioned in it.

1. A deliberate contrast between prophecy and tongues structures the whole chapter. This pairing runs like a backbone down the body of almost the entire argument: verses 2 and 3 ("One who speaks in a tongue does not speak to men, but to God; . . . but one who prophesies speaks to men"), verse 4 ("one who speaks in a tongue edifies himself; but one who prophesies edifies the church"), verse 5 ("I wish that you all spoke in tongues, but even more that you would prophesy"; again, "greater is one who prophesies than one who speaks in tongues . . . "), verse 6 (" . . . if I come to you speaking in tongues, what shall I profit you, unless I speak to you by way of . . . prophecy . . . ?"), verses 7–19 (detailed discussion of tongues, particularly their unintelligibility apart from interpretation), verse 22, following out of the command and appeal to the Old Testament in verses 20, 21 ("tongues are a sign, not for believers but for unbelievers; prophecy is for believers, not for unbelievers"), verses 23 and 24 ("if the whole church comes together and all speak in tongues, . . . but if all prophesy . . . "), directions concerning the exercise, in the congregational assembly, of tongues (vv. 27f.) and prophecy (vv. 29–32), verse 39, the capstone of the discussion ("desire to prophesy, and do not forbid speaking in tongues").

2. Within this dominating contrast, prophecy is the superior element, tongues the subordinate element (see especially vv. 1c, 5a, and 39). Throughout the chapter tongues show the relatively greater importance of prophecy or, conversely, prophecy shows the relative inferiority of tongues. At any rate, the main point of the chapter is the relative superiority of prophecy to tongues (see also the note on which the chapter opens and closes, vv. 1, 39).

We may for a moment dip into the background at Corinth, which is notoriously difficult to recapture in detail. The apparent reason for Paul's emphasis and pattern of argumentation is that some in the congregation had reversed priorities, holding tongues to be superior to prophecy, or perhaps even took the position that tongues are the only appropriate mode of prophecy. Paul agrees that a sharp division between the two is not possible; both are associated with the reception and communication of "mysteries" (13:2 and 14:2). But he is deeply concerned to make clear to the

Corinthians the difference between the two phenomena and, as we have seen, the relative superiority of prophecy to tongues.

3. Prophecy is superior or preferable to tongues, particularly in view of the principle of edification that controls the exercise of all gifts (see above, pp. 49f.). Only prophecy edifies others in the church (v. 4).

4. Tongues, however, are to be interpreted (vv. 13, 26; cf. v. 5; 12:10) and, when interpreted, are functionally equivalent to prophecy in that both edify the church (v. 5). Whether and in what respects this equivalence extends further may remain an open question for the present. In any case the fundamental inferiority or depreciation of tongues relative to prophecy apparently applies only to *uninterpreted* tongues and is removed when interpretation takes place. The generalization of verse 5b ("one who prophesies is greater than one who speaks in tongues") holds only when tongues are uninterpreted. Interpreted tongues, then, are on a more or less equal footing with prophecy, although it seems difficult to evade as an overriding suggestion of the passage, underlying the concluding injunction (v. 39), that prophecy is more useful and efficient because it doesn't require interpretation to edify.

5. Prophecy and tongues belong together and are complementary in their exercise. While Paul does somewhat flexibly associate prophecy with all speech "with the mind" (v. 19), it would be wrong to suppose that his argument would remain substantially the same, if throughout he had substituted teaching, say, for prophecy, or that his purposes would have been just as well served by arguing that teaching (or any other ministry involving intelligible words) edifies the church but tongues, if uninterpreted, do not. His concern is with *both* prophecy and tongues, their proper place and exercise, and their *relationship* to each other. The close tie between them is seen not only in the sustained contrast, already noted, which structures the entire chapter, but also in the parallel sets of directives concerning their exercise (cf. vv. 27f. with 29–32): the need for similar ordering ("two or at the

most three") and for correlative interpretation/discernment (note also the apparent correlation of these gifts, respectively, with tongues and prophecy in 12:10). This tie and these parallels reflect, in turn, as I will try to show below, close similarities between prophecy and tongues both in the Spirit-worked origin and the content of each.

Tongues are tied to prophecy and stand, so to speak, in its shadow. There is at least the suggestion in the chapter that tongues have no place in the life of the congregation apart from their coexistence and correlative exercise with prophecy. If there are considerations that offset this coexistence, they are certainly not spelled out in this passage.

6. What ties prophecy and tongues together, what they have in common that makes them comparable (contrastable) and explains their functional equivalence, is that both are *word*-gifts.

Against the background of this overview of I Corinthians 14, what more precisely is the nature of each of these word-gifts?

B. Prophecy (the Christian prophet)

Current discussions about the role of the New Testament prophet are widespread and have resulted in considerable differences of opinion. These differences, for one thing, no doubt stem from the difficulty of having to reconstruct a coherent overall picture from somewhat disparate materials, found almost entirely in Acts, Paul, and Revelation. Inevitably, then, conclusions reached are influenced by the weight and evaluation given these materials relative to each other. Accordingly, I want to make clear that our discussion here is controlled by the following assumptions: (1) what Paul says in I Corinthians 12–14 applies to prophecy as a *whole*, in *all* its aspects, as it functioned at Corinth; (2) granting relative differences in the prominence of a particular aspect from place to place, as a whole prophecy at Corinth was not different but the same phenomenon, unified in its various aspects, present in other congregations mentioned elsewhere in Paul, and in Acts and Revelation. This means that, while the discussion of I Corinthians 12–14 is certainly the most extensive, we must give passages elsewhere their due in reconstructing the role of the Corinthian prophets (as typical of prophets in other congregations), rather than concluding, when these other passages clash with a picture derived exclusively from I Corinthians, that they present a different "kind" or diverging conception of prophecy.

To balance our discussion as a whole, we should recognize first of all that according to the New Testament *all* believers are prophets; the whole church is a congregation of prophets. Analogous to the Reformation insistence on the universal priesthood of believers, we may speak of the "prophethood" of all within the new covenant community, in the sense that the words of God (cf. Rom. 3:2) are accessible to all, and that by the Spirit's work the laws and statutes of the covenant are a testimony written in the hearts and manifested in the lives of all (cf., e.g., Isa. 59:21; Jer. 31:33; Ezek. 36:27; II Cor. 3:3ff.; I John 2:27).

Apparently without exception, however, the New Testament vocabulary for prophecy is not used in this sense. There, applied to the church, it refers to a gift or function having two basic characteristics: (1) it is a gift given only to some, not all, in the church; it is a gift present on the principle of differential distribution; (2) it is a revelatory gift; that is, it brings to the church the words of God in the primary and original sense. Prophecy is not, at least primarily or as one of its necessary marks, the interpretation of an already existing inspired text or oral tradition but is itself the inspired, nonderivative word of God.

In important respects, then, there is close continuity with both the Old Testament prophets and the New Testament apostles. Apparently the designation *prophet* is applied to those who exercise the gift frequently or with some regularity (e.g., Acts 21:10; I Cor. 12:28), while the gift itself can function temporarily in others on particular occasions (see Acts 19:6—also perhaps Acts 21:9; I Cor. 11:4f.).

This basic profile of New Testament prophecy can be substantiated and various objections to it discussed by examining relevant passages more carefully.

1. In I Corinthians 12–14 prophecy is obviously a gift given only to some in the church (12:10, 28, 29, as well other indications throughout the passage). That this is also the case in other situations follows from Romans 12:6 and Ephesians 4:11.

Also, its revelatory character is apparent. **(a)** True, Paul does associate prophecy with all intelligible speech (14:19; cf. the connection with teaching, v. 6), but the element of revelation is plainly at its core. This can be seen in verse 30—"If a revelation comes to another [prophet; cf. vv. 29, 31] . . ."—and verse 26. The latter functions to introduce a section (through v. 33) concerned with ordering the worship of the assembly. Since prophecy is not mentioned explicitly among the elements listed, yet the following verses are taken up entirely with regulating prophecy along with tongues, it seems fair to conclude that prophecy is being included in some way in verse 26. Specifically, in the light of verse 30, "a revelation" is a variant reference to prophecy. Note, too, the sequence in verse 26: "a revelation" is followed directly by "a tongue, or an interpretation," reflecting the correlation between prophecy and tongues that dominates the chapter. This suggests further that verse 6b does not list four distinct gifts but that there "revelation" (and "knowledge," cf. 13:2, 8) and "prophecy" define each other. At any rate, in these instances (vv. 26 and 30) the revelation in view does not result from the general working of the Spirit as the "Spirit of wisdom and revelation" (Eph. 1:17, NIV), given to all believers (cf. Phil. 3:15), but is a specific revelation given by inspiration to one for the edification of others.

(b) Another indication of the revelatory character of prophecy is found in the association of prophecy with knowing "all mysteries" (13:2). The composition of the conditional clauses in verses 1–3 is as follows:

"if I speak with the tongues of men and of angels, . . . " (1)

"if I have the gift of prophecy, and know all mysteries and all knowledge; . . . " (2a)

"if I have all faith, so as to remove mountains, . . . " (2b)

"if I give away all I possess, . . . " (3a)

"if I surrender my body to be burned, . . . " (3b)

The repetition of "if" (ἐάν) would seem to mark off from each other the different gifts Paul selects to illustrate the futility of exercising any gift without love. In verse 2a, then, the bracketing together in one clause of knowing mysteries and knowledge with prophecy shows at the very least that the former, if a distinct gift, corresponds closely to the latter. More likely, however, mysteries and knowledge spell out the content of prophecy.

Elsewhere in Paul "mystery" is one of the central categories of revelation, accenting that what is revealed is hidden and inaccessible to man apart from the sovereign, unilateral disclosure of God. Its content is not some esoteric body of cryptic truths but the eschatological salvation revealed in Christ. The term either refers to that salvation comprehensively (Rom. 16:25; Eph. 1:9; 3:3ff.; 6:19; Col. 1:26, 27; 2:2; 4:3), or to specific aspects related to it (see especially the *prophecies* in Rom. 11:25ff.; I Cor. 15:51ff.).

The mystery is the revealed mystery that has been made known to the nations by apostolic proclamation (Rom. 16:25; Eph. 3:9; Col. 1:25f.) and is "the mystery of the gospel" (Eph. 6:19), "the mystery of Christ" (Col. 4:3), possessed by all believers. It might be argued, then, that I Corinthians 13:2 says no more than that the prophets here in view express (in some distinctive, spontaneous way) what is already possessed and known in common by the church. Such reasoning, however, overlooks that this reference is like the usage in Romans 11:25ff. and I Corinthians 15:51ff., where "mystery" is a particular revelation previously unknown and now given and communicated for the first time. This understanding accords better with the description of prophecy and the activity of the prophet in 14:26 and 30 and is also confirmed by the plural, "mysteries," which accents the specific and nonderivative nature of the revelations involved.

2. What Paul says in Ephesians 3:3–5 reinforces and focuses our conclusions from I Corinthians 12–14. My assumption here, to be demonstrated below (pp. 93–95), is that verse 5 (cf. 2:20) has in view the New Testament prophets as a group distinct from both the apostles and Old Testament prophets. In a context where he is surveying his ministry in the broadest and most fundamental terms, Paul grounds that ministry in the fact that "the mystery was made known to me by revelation" (v. 3). This mystery, he goes on to explain, is "the mystery of Christ" (v. 4) in all its

fulness (cf. vv. 8, 16–19), the mystery, "which was not made known to men in other generations as it has now been revealed by the Spirit to His holy apostles and prophets" (v. 5).

In view of the sweeping outlook of this passage, the conclusions that can be drawn from it are fundamental to an overall understanding of prophecy in the New Testament. There is no warrant, for instance, for supposing that Paul has in view the Ephesian prophets in distinction from the Corinthian prophets. (a) The revelation granted to and made known by the New Testament prophets is on a par and of one piece with the inspired revelation received and proclaimed by Paul and the other apostles. (b) This prophetic revelation is not addressed to individualistic, purely localized interests, but concerns, along with apostolic revelation, the salvation in Christ with its rich and manifold implications for the faith and life of the church (cf. vv. 8–10).

3. In Romans 12:6, Paul writes: "If [one's gift is] prophecy, [let him prophesy] according to the proportion of his faith." The meaning of the prepositional phrase is a matter of some dispute. One view takes it to mean, as a literal translation might suggest, "according to the analogy of the faith," "analogy" being understood as a rule or norm and "the faith" as the objective deposit of revelation in the church (for the use of "faith" in this sense, see, e.g., Acts 6:7; I Tim. 5:8; Jude 3). The thought, then, would be that prophecy is to conform to the truth already revealed to the church.

Almost certainly, however, the phrase describes, as all the standard English translations render it, the proportion or measure of the prophet's own faith. Its sense is close to "measure of faith" in verse 3. There (vv. 3, 4) Paul, in beginning his comments on various gifts operative in the church at Rome (vv. 3–8), says in effect that "sound judgment" is bound to recognize that the particular allotment of faith which God has apportioned to each member of Christ's body is the reason why all the members do not have the same function. Differences in function within the church rest on differences in the way faith is apportioned. This corresponds closely to the beginning of verse 6: believers have different gifts according to the grace given to each.

"Measure of faith" obviously does not mean that faith is a quantity that can be divided up and distributed in portions. Nor is the thought that saving faith varies from believer to believer as if some share more, others less, in Christ and his righteousness. The New Testament could not teach more plainly that by faith all believers, without exception, are united to Christ and so have his perfect righteousness accounted to them (see, e.g., Rom. 3:21—5:21; Gal. 2:15—4:7). And nowhere does the New Testament teach that the possession of a particular gift depends on the strength of saving faith or a relatively greater manifestation of the "fruit of the Spirit" (Gal. 5:22f.), which inevitably accompanies that faith. (Paul's point is just the opposite in I Corinthians 13, discussed below: the possession of one or more gifts is not necessarily evidence of a strong faith active in love.)

Rather, in this passage "faith" is correlative with "grace" and "gift," and that correlation determines its precise, restricted sense here. The way in which the latter two words are used (v. 6) to describe the differing gifts graciously distributed in the church explains how "faith" can be the believer's faith (his believing) and yet differ "in measure" from believer to believer. This passage contains the always pertinent reminder of the vital role of faith, not only in our becoming members of Christ's body but also in the continuing use of specific functions allotted to each of us as members of the body. No gift is rightly exercised apart from faith.

Accordingly, as the gifts in the body are different, so the faith of the recipients differs in respect to what distinguishes the exercise of a particular gift from others; the recipient's faith *as expressed in that exercise* is different. As the gifts of believers differ, so in each instance the corresponding "measure of faith" differs. "Faith" here is grace, that is, the various gifts, particularly their appropriate exercise, viewed from the side of the recipients. This understanding of the correlation between gift (grace) and faith is confirmed by indications in the other two lists of gifts in Paul, especially Ephesians 4:7, where Paul says: "To each one of us grace was given according to the measure of Christ's gift," NASB (note the explanation of this statement in terms of gifts [v. 8] variously distributed [v. 11] in the church). The "measure of

Christ's gift" is the "measure of faith." "Measure," "proportion,"
and "varieties" (I Cor. 12:4–6) have an interchangeable reference
in these passages.

Romans 12:6b, then, notes the distribution, according to grace,
of different gifts (faith) in the specific instance of prophecy. The
"proportion of faith" (v. 6) is the "measure of faith" (v. 3), par-
ticularized for prophecy and the regulation of its exercise. This
helps to understand the trend of the passage as a whole, especially
the unusual composition of verses 6b–8, which, at least initially,
can seem awkward and disjointed in their flow. In view of the
controlling "measure of faith [grace]" principle (vv. 3, 6a), after
Paul in fact begins, "If [one's gift is] prophecy, [let him use it]
according to the proportion of his faith," he could have continued,
"If [one's gift is] service, [let him use it] according to the proportion of his faith; if teaching, according to the proportion of
his faith; if exhorting, according to the proportion of his faith";
etc. Alternatively, in terms of the same controlling principle,
he could have begun, "If [one's gift is] prophecy, [let him use
it] in prophesying," just as he in fact continues, "If [one's gift
is] service, [let him use it] in serving; if teaching, in teaching;
if exhorting, in exhorting"; etc. The overriding consideration of
the passage is the faithful and appropriate exercise of each of the
different gifts graciously given to the one body in Christ.

The important point, finally, is that whether "proportion [anal-
ogy] of faith" refers to (1) the objective deposit of revealed truth
or, as I have been arguing, (2) the prophet's own (exercise of)
faith, it does not imply the subjective, nonrevelatory character of
prophecy, in part or as a whole, or a relativizing of the prophet's
authority. In alternative (1), the prophet is being exhorted that the
revelation given through him must accord with previous revelations to the church, just as Peter needed to be exhorted that his
conduct as an apostle, at Antioch, must not contradict what had
already been revealed to and taught by him and others (Gal.
2:11–14; cf. Acts 10:9–16, 28f., 34ff.; 11:4ff.). In the second, much
more likely alternative, the prophet is being exhorted to the faithful and appropriate use of his gift, subject to his control (cf. I Cor.
14:32), just as Peter needed to be exhorted to the consistent and
proper exercise of his apostleship. Nothing in Romans 12:6

suggests that prophecy is anything less than the word of God in the primary, original sense. Contrary points of view rest on a misunderstanding of the need for discrimination and evaluation with reference to prophecy (I Cor. 12:10; 14:29), to be discussed below.

4. The Book of Acts, particularly the case of Agabus, is instructive concerning the origin and character of prophetic revelation.

a. In 21:10, 11, Agabus, identified as a prophet, comes down from Judea to Caesarea, takes Paul's belt, binds his own hands and feet with it and says, "Thus says the Holy Spirit, 'In this way the Jews at Jerusalem will bind the owner of this belt and hand him over to the Gentiles.'"

In the plainest possible terms, here the words of Agabus in his identity as a prophet are the words of the Holy Spirit himself, a quote of what the Spirit says. Not only what the prophet receives but what he says and communicates to others is inspired revelation. The correspondence to Old Testament prophecy is conspicuous: the use of the introductory formula with "Holy Spirit" substituted for "Lord," prediction, and an accompanying symbolic act (cf., e.g., Isa. 20:2–6). Just as in the Old Testament, this does not mean that every prophecy conformed to this pattern or involved prediction. But there is no good reason to suppose that this incident is not typical or not indicative of the origin and character of New Testament prophecy.

This incident, particularly if it is recognized as typical, is a strong piece of evidence. The effort is sometimes made to undercut it by maintaining that Agabus presumptuously overstepped himself in speaking for the Holy Spirit and was unmasked by the subsequent course of events, since Paul was not handed over to the Romans by the Jerusalem Jews, as Agabus predicted, but was rescued from a murderous Jewish mob and imprisoned by the Romans (21:27ff.).

Against this construction in general is the pedantic precision it demands from Agabus' prediction. Predictive prophecy can of course be exact and detailed but is not necessarily so. Moreover, after the fact, Paul echoes the language of Agabus by telling the Jews at Rome, "I was arrested in Jerusalem and handed over to the

Romans" (Acts 28:17, NIV). To argue from the particulars of the Greek text that Paul focuses here on the one detail of his transfer from (Roman imprisonment in) Jerusalem to the Roman authorities in Caesarea (23:23ff.) is to miss the plainly summary nature of his remark in the immediate context and to be guilty of the same overly pedantic demand placed on Agabus. Also, there is nothing in Paul's immediate reaction (21:13: "I am ready not only to be bound, but also to die in Jerusalem for the name of the Lord Jesus") that suggests any inaccuracy in Agabus' prophecy. It is, and is recorded by Luke as, an accurate forecast of what actually transpired: the hostility of the Jerusalem Jews deprived Paul of his freedom and forced him into Roman custody.

Another point sometimes raised is that the urging of those present, including Luke, that Paul not go up to Jerusalem (Acts 21:12), indicates that Agabus' words are not without reservation the words of the Holy Spirit. But this resistance to Agabus' pronouncement, even if he himself was involved, no more shows that its origin was less than fully divine than Peter's withdrawal from table-fellowship with Gentiles (Gal. 2:11ff.) shows that the origin and authority of the "call nothing unclean" vision given to him at Joppa (Acts 10:9–16; cf. v. 23) were less than fully divine. The measure of the authenticity and authority of a revelation is not the (inappropriate) response(s) to it.

This incident at Caesarea helps us to understand what took place a short while earlier at Tyre, when "through the Spirit" the disciples urged Paul not to go to Jerusalem (21:4). Again, Luke's point is not the impaired validity and unreliability of their speech, in which nevertheless the Spirit is somehow instrumental, but their recoil against what the Spirit had revealed to them of Paul's future. That revelation and their response to it must not be confused or merged in their speech-act. Both events—at Caesarea and Tyre—are part of the larger picture toward the close of Paul's third missionary journey, where, as Paul is compelled on to Jerusalem by the Spirit, "in every city the Holy Spirit warns me that prison and hardships are facing me" (20:22f., NIV).

The activity of Agabus is mentioned earlier by Luke in 11:27, 28, where, identified as one of a group of prophets come down from Jerusalem to Antioch, "he predicted through the Spirit that a severe famine would spread over the entire [Roman] world." The fully inspired character of Agabus' words is sometimes denied by alleging an imprecise sense for the Greek verb ("vaguely indicated") and a looser connection between the Spirit's work and what was said. This effort, however, dissolves, both in the more explicit description of Agabus' activity in 21:11, already examined, and the prosaic way in which Luke here records the fulfillment of Agabus' prophecy ("This happened during the reign of Claudius"). The tenor of his report is this: the Spirit predicted it, and that's what happened.

b. A couple of other passages on the activity of prophets in Acts fill out and reinforce the picture already sketched. According to 13:1, 2, while the "prophets and teachers" at Antioch were serving the Lord and fasting, "the Holy Spirit said, 'Set apart for me Barnabas and Saul for the work to which I have called them'" (13:1f.). It would no doubt be unwarranted to insist that these words of the Spirit, which authorized and initiated the first missionary journey (cf. v. 4), were given to and spoken by one or more of the prophets mentioned in verse 1. Yet that possibility, in the light of what we have already seen in Acts, is very much a live one and can't be excluded.

In Acts 15:32, the prophets Judas and Silas, having been sent to Antioch along with Paul and Barnabas to communicate the letter containing the decision of the Jerusalem Council (vv. 22, 27), encourage and strengthen the brothers in Antioch at length. The question can be left open here as to just why their identity as prophets is accented ("being prophets also themselves"). Perhaps it is because Paul and Barnabas, whom they accompany, are prophets (cf. 13:2, but also 14:4, 14), or to point out that their message of encouragement is as inspired and authoritative as that of Paul and Barnabas. Or to indicate the prophetic character of the decision reached by the Council and of the letter sent to Antioch, and perhaps also to intimate their own prominent role at the Council (cf. v. 22: "leading men among the brothers"). At any rate this verse shows that the activity of the prophet is hortatory or at least involves a hortatory element. The description here fits Paul's generalization (I Cor. 14:3): the one who prophesies speaks for strengthening, exhortation, comfort. On the basis of what we have seen so far there is no warrant for distinguishing two separate kinds or classes of prophets (prophecy) in the New Testament. That is, there is no reason to distinguish between the Corinthian prophets and the prophets in Acts, or between the inspired prophecy of prediction and the uninspired prophecy of exhortation.

5. The Book of Revelation itself is a massive example of Christian prophecy. While the author (John) does not call himself a prophet, that is the plain implication. The whole is repeatedly and explicitly termed a prophecy, both at the beginning and the end: "the words of the prophecy" (1:3), "the words of the prophecy of this book" (22:7, 10, 18), "the words of the book of this prophecy" (22:19). As such, it is a "revelation of Jesus Christ," that is, a revelation from Christ to his servants (1:1), "the word of God," "the testimony of Jesus Christ" (1:2; cf. v. 9). It reports the words of the ascended Christ (1:11, 17ff.), which at the same time are "what the Spirit says to the churches." The invariable pattern of the letters to the seven churches is that each opens as what the exalted Christ, variously described, says (2:1, 8, 12, 18; 3:1, 7, 14) and closes as what the Spirit says (2:7, 11, 17, 29; 3:6, 13, 22). The prophetic message of Revelation is the word of the glorified Christ, the life-giving Spirit.

It has been held that Revelation as prophecy is on a higher level of inspiration and authority than other New Testament prophecy. This position depends on the assumption that prophecy elsewhere in the New Testament has a lower authority or that the rest of the New Testament makes a distinction between prophecy with and without binding authority, an assumption which we have tried to show is without support.

Nor does Revelation itself support a distinction between different levels of prophetic authority. Unambiguous references to New Testament prophecy are few, but what slight evidence there is points in the opposite direction. In 22:9 the angel tells John, "I am a fellow servant with you and with your brothers the prophets and of all who keep the words of this book." Parallel to this, in 19:10 the angel says to John, "I am a fellow servant with you and with your brothers who have the testimony of Jesus." In the light of distinctions made elsewhere—saints and prophets (16:6; cf. 11:18; 18:24), saints and apostles and prophets (18:20)—"your brothers the prophets" in 22:9 does not refer to all believers (as his brothers; cf. 1:9) but to a group seen together with John in distinction from other believers. In all likelihood, then, this group of prophets is "your brothers who have the testimony of Jesus" in 19:10.

There the angel adds, "For the testimony of Jesus is the Spirit of prophecy." In the light of its occurrence elsewhere (1:2, 9; 12:17; 20:4) "the testimony of Jesus" is not witness to or about Jesus, but witness borne by Jesus, Jesus' own witness. The apparent sense of this admittedly difficult addition is that the testimony given by Jesus to John and his (prophet-) brothers is inspired prophecy. The words of the exalted Jesus through the prophets are the words of the Spirit (cf. chaps. 2 and 3). Revelation 12:17 does say that all believers "have the testimony of Jesus." But this does not demand the conclusion that the prophets are not in view in 19:10 or that there is after all no real distinction between prophets and other believers in possessing and communicating the testimony of Jesus. Rather, all believers have the testimony of Jesus derivatively from John and the (other) prophets to whom it has first been given (1:9; 19:10) by the Spirit of prophecy.

At any rate, 22:9 plainly associates the prophets together with John as his brothers in distinction from other believers, an association pointing to common prophetic function and authority. The fact that he expects them to acknowledge and submit to his prophecy (22:18f.) does not mean that the authority of their prophecies is lower in principle, any more than Paul's demand that Peter submit to his teaching (Gal. 2:11ff.) means that his teaching authority was superior to that of the other apostles (cf. vv. 7–9). Nor does the written character of Revelation as prophecy give it greater authority than the oral deliverances of the prophets, any more than the teachings (traditions) of the apostles have more authority in writing than orally (see especially II Thess. 2:15). These observations, by the way, apply equally to Paul's regulation of the Corinthian prophets, including the strongly-worded command of I Corinthians 14:37, 38. This controlling of their activities does not mean that what they spoke was not the authoritative word of God. The issue ultimately is the authority of God's word, whoever it may be that speaks (writes) it. A distinction between absolute and relative prophetic authority can be found in Revelation only by reading that distinction into it from the outside.

6. In I Corinthians 12:10 Paul associates with prophecy the gift of discerning or distinguishing between spirits, apparently in parallel to the gift of interpretation connected with tongues. Similarly, in 14:29 he commands that what the prophets say be weighed or evaluated by "the others." The latter expression may refer to the rest of the entire congregation, not just the other prophets. But even if that be the case, in view of the parallel sequence in 12:10 (i.e., prophecy, discriminating ability; tongues, interpretation) and the parallel regulation of tongues and prophecy in 14:27ff. ("two or three," followed by interpretation/evaluation), those who have the gift of discernment mentioned in 12:10 certainly play a leading role in the evaluation process.

Appeal is sometimes made to the need for this complementary gift, to show that New Testament prophecy, at least at Corinth and Thessalonica (I Thess. 5:20f.), is a kind of low-level "revelation" lacking the full authority of the Word of God, a mixing of revelatory and nonrevelatory elements whose resultant authority is ambiguous. Such a viewpoint not only disregards the fully inspired, revelatory character of prophecy already noted but misses the point of this companion gift. The distinguishing or discrimination required functions to determine the source of an alleged prophecy, whether or not it is genuine, whether it is from the Holy Spirit or some other spirit; it does not sift worthwhile elements presumably based on a revelation from those that are not. Perhaps also included is an interpretive function, assessing in some way the significance of the prophecy for the congregation.

This evaluating function is also expressed in general terms in I John 4:1: "Do not believe every spirit, but test the spirits to see whether they are from God, because many false prophets have gone out into the world." In the context the central issue is confession of the fully incarnate reality of Jesus' coming and continuing existence (v. 2; cf. 5:6), quite similar, by the way, to Paul's concern in I Corinthians 12 with confession of (the *incarnate*)

Jesus as exalted Lord (v. 3). The Thessalonian correspondence provides an instructive example of what is involved. The command to "test everything" (I Thessalonians 5:21, the same verb used in I John 4:1), including prophecies (v. 20), bears specifically on avoiding the confusion created by a "spirit" ("prophecy," NIV) to the effect that the day of the Lord has already come (II Thessalonians 2:2). This also shows, since Paul mentions this disturbing "spirit" in parallel with a letter supposedly from him, that he is concerned about false prophecy and the spurious misuse of the prophetic gift *within* the church.

What also needs to be grasped is that in the case of genuine prophecies, the need for evaluation does not show that they lack the full authority of God's Word. Rather, this evaluation is of a piece with the positive proving, the affirmative testing Paul the apostle commands for his own teaching (again, with the same verb [δοκιμάζω] used in I Thess. 5:21; I John 4:1) in Romans 12:2 and Ephesians 5:10 (cf. Gal. 1:8): "prove what the will of God is, what is good, pleasing and perfect," "prove what is pleasing to the Lord." Again, I Thessalonians 5:19–22 is instructive: "Do not quench the Spirit; do not despise prophecies; but test everything; hold fast to what is good; avoid every kind of evil." A most likely understanding of these verses is that they are a unit, with the movement of thought from the general to the specific and back to the general: from inspired utterance of every kind, none of which is to be rejected, to prophecy in particular, which is not to be despised (perhaps reflecting the depreciation of prophecy in relation to other gifts, like tongues, in Thessalonica, as in Corinth), back to the testing of all inspired utterance (including but not restricted to prophecies), holding to what is genuine and refusing the spurious. Appropriate to prophecy as well as the inspired preaching of the apostles, no more and no less, is the response of the Bereans, who "received the word with great eagerness and examined the Scriptures daily to see whether these things were so" (Acts 17:11).

7. Conclusion: This survey of prophecy in the New Testament has not been exhaustive, either in examining all the relevant passages or in discussing those passages examined. My intention has been to sketch a picture that will remain essentially unchanged by more detailed investigation and the answers to whatever questions have been left open here. That picture is as follows: New Testament prophecy is revelatory. The issue is not whether or to what extent prophetic revelations are "new" in the sense of disclosing content not previously revealed (any more than, say, a given passage in Luke is not fully revelatory because a parallel is found in [presumably earlier] Mark). Rather, the issue is the inspired, Spirit-worked origin of prophecy and its correlative authority. The words of the prophet are the words of God and are to be received and responded to as such.

In general, the prophets are associated with the apostles in disclosing to the church the "unsearchable riches" and "manifold wisdom" of the mystery revealed in Christ (Eph. 3:5, 8–10). (This association will be further clarified below.) Prophetic revelation of the mystery involves both "forthtelling" (e.g., Acts 15:32; I Cor. 14:3) and "foretelling" (e.g., Acts 11:28; 21:10). There is no warrant for finding in these two broad functions a distinction between two essentially different kinds of prophecy, whereby the former ("forthtelling") lacks the fully inspired origin and authority of the Word of God. Leaving room for differences in the actual outworking and relative prominence of these two functions from place to place, the material in Acts and Paul provides a picture of a single, unified prophetic activity present in the various church centers (Antioch, Ephesus, Corinth, Thessalonica, and elsewhere) mentioned in the New Testament, and that picture is one of marked continuity with both the apostles and the Old Testament prophets.

Our conclusion can be summarized in terms of the fundamental difference between preaching (teaching) and prophecy. Nonprophetic proclamation is based on a *text*; it receives its legitimation as (proper) *interpretation* of the inscripturated Word of God or, as the case may be, at the time the New Testament was being written, authoritative, apostolic oral tradition. Prophetic proclamation, in contrast, is Spirit-worked speech of such a quality that its authority resides just in that inspired origin. A basic difference between prophecy and preaching is that the prophet has no text. The prophet reveals the Word of God, the preacher expounds that Word.

C. Tongues

Earlier in this chapter (section A) we noticed the sustained connection between prophecy and tongues in I Corinthians 14. Turning now to the other side of that tie we begin by examining what Paul says about (1) the origin and (2) the content of tongues.

1. The most pronounced indication of the origin of tongues is found in verse 14, which is usually translated: "For if I pray in a tongue, my spirit prays, but my mind is unfruitful." In exercising the gift of tongues the mind of the speaker is bypassed ("unfruitful"), at the very least in the sense that his mind is not used in the production of the speech, probably also in the sense that he himself does not understand what is being said, that is, does not apprehend it with his mind. Throughout this passage (vv. 15–19; cf. 7–11) the mind is the proper locus of language, if language is understood as the vehicle for intelligible communication; language is a capacity of the mind, and understanding and cognitive meaning are functions of the mind, or at least involve the mind. But Paul says that the mind of the tongues-speaker is not involved in what he says. Whether or not to exercise the gift as to time and place, but not the speaking itself, is subject to control by his mind (v. 28; cf. 19, 23).

Verse 14, then, says either that the vocalization of the tongues-speaker involves the Spirit's use of some aspect of his personality other than the mind or that his person is completely bypassed except for the utilization of his voice, his sound-producing mechanisms, by the Spirit. In various forms the first viewpoint is widely held today. According to this view tongues are not the words of the Holy Spirit but a Spirit-worked vocalizing of a volitional, yet non-intellective, preconceptual capacity in man, usually with the emphasis that tongues bring to expression the more primal, deeper levels of personality, that in man which is more genuinely and authentically human. Tongues enable one to express concerns resident in the deepest recesses of his being, concerns otherwise suppressed and inhibited by the superficialities of conceptualization and conventional language. In other words, this view, whether or not explicitly and consciously, takes "my spirit" (v. 14) anthro-

pologically, as referring to the human spirit, spirit as an aspect
of man.

a. But this—what to many may seem self-evident—is one of the
great, perhaps insuperable difficulties with this position exegetically. To take the contrast between "mind" and "spirit" in verses
14–19 as the contrast between the nonintellective, preconceptual
and rational, cognitive sides of man is without support elsewhere
in Paul. In fact, it is foreign not only to Paul but the entire New
Testament teaching about man. Paul's anthropology can be sur-
veyed by means of the basic distinction between "the inner man"
and "the outer man" (II Cor. 4:16; cf. Rom. 7:22; Eph. 3:16). In terms
of this distinction, (human) "spirit" (πνεῦμα) and "mind" (νοῦς)
both pertain to the inner man. As such, both terms overlap in
meaning and have essentially the same reference, along with
"heart" (καρδία) and "soul" (ψυχή). Specifically, these terms refer
to man's "center," what in his make-up most deeply determines his
thinking and acting.

For example, this overlap can be seen in Romans 1:9 (". . . God,
whom I serve in my spirit in preaching the gospel of his Son. . . "),
where Paul's "service" of God with his *spirit* is realized in the
(*intelligible*) word-ministry of gospel-preaching. As such it is but
one instance of the "spiritual [rational, λογικήν] service" (Rom.
12:1) incumbent on all believers, which results from the "renew-
ing of the *mind*" (v. 2). Again, Paul exhorts the Corinthians, for
the sake of the gospel, to be united "in the same mind" (I Cor.
1:10; cf. vv. 13–17), while, in encouraging the Philippians to conduct themselves in a manner worthy of the gospel, he hopes to
hear that they are standing firm "in one spirit," contending "with
one mind [ψυχῇ]" (Phil. 1:27). Ephesians 4:23 is particularly instructive: the comprehensive renewal realized by putting on the
new man in Christ (v. 24) is renewal that takes place "in the spirit
of your mind." This expression can be read only as a compound-
ing of anthropological terms (cf., e.g., I Thess. 5:23: "spirit and
soul") to emphasize the thorough transformation of the inner
man. It shows that "spirit" and "mind" are basically synonymous
("the attitude of your minds," NIV), or at least that they are not set
over against each other as contrasting parts of the personality.
Further, the center of man's *comprehensive* searching and self-

knowledge is his spirit, analogous to the activity of the Spirit of God in God (I Cor. 2:10f.). And the (intelligible) joint-witness of the Spirit with the believer's spirit is that he is God's child, resulting in the (comprehensible) cry to God as Father (Rom. 8:15f.). Finally, the typical closing benediction, "The grace of the Lord Jesus Christ be with your spirit" (Gal. 6:18; Phil. 4:23; II Tim. 4:22; Philem. 25), is directed not just to one aspect but to the whole man in terms of the integrating center of all his functions. The picture in the rest of the New Testament only confirms what we find in Paul (cf., e.g., Acts 18:25, where Apollos' "fervency in spirit" is expressed by the intelligible activity of "speaking and teaching accurately the things concerning Jesus"): man's spirit does not have functions in contrast to his mind, but is, like his mind, his inner life in its (intended) wholeness and integrity.

The view, then, that the contrast in I Corinthians 14:14 is between the cognitive and preconceptual sides of man is foreign to the New Testament. Where then does it come from? No doubt a number of factors explain such a widespread viewpoint, but a basic one, it seems to me, is its reaction against a secularized use of reason. The assertion of rational autonomy, which has become dominant in the West, especially since the Enlightenment, has now, in the twentieth century, been increasingly unmasked in its deepest intention and outworkings. It threatens to devour man and destroy his integrity, and so efforts are being made to offset and balance it by emphasizing the irrational and nonconceptual in man, for the recapture of the self in its wholeness.

There is every biblical warrant for opposing this dehumanizing exercise of reason, as it works itself out, for instance, in a depersonalizing use of technology or an inappropriate and destructive application of mechanistic models to various areas of human experience. But the solution does not lie in building on the conviction that religious experience is essentially irrational and that man's nonrational and preconceptual capacities are the proper sphere of the Spirit's working, the locus of his direct activity in man. That conviction only compounds the confusion because it does not really challenge man's rebellious pretensions to rational autonomy but at best only relativizes them. It makes room for religious experience but without recapturing the wholeness it is seeking, because it leaves reason essentially untouched and secularized and so ends up only intensifying tensions and splits in human experience. The Bible wishes to know only of the whole man and his love for God, with mind as well as heart, soul, and strength (Mark 12:30), of the worshipful offering to God of the entire self (body), controlled by a renewed mind (Rom. 12:1f.). To be sure, the Bible also knows about the limitations of our language and conceptualizing capacities, particularly when it comes to God and ourselves and our inevitable relationship to him. The gift of salvation in Christ is "unspeakable," indescribable, beyond words (II Cor. 9:15). The joy of Christians is "inexpressible" (I Peter 1:8); so too are aspects of God's revelation (II Cor. 12:4). In their full scope his judgments are unsearchable and his ways cannot be fathomed (Rom. 11:33). But Scripture never gives any indication that the impenetrable greatness of God and the incomprehensible depths of his love are better grasped and articulated by some other, allegedly deeper aspect of personality than the mind with its language capacities. Man is more than his mind; he is not an intellectualistic machine. But this "more" is not inevitably in tension with the mind, nor does language necessarily distort or obscure the wholeness of experience. The limitation that confronts us here is not that of one part of man (mind) relative to some other (spirit), but the limitations of the whole man, the creature, in all his functions before his Creator.

b. But now if verse 14 does not contrast the mind of the believer with his (human) spirit, how then is it to be understood, particularly "my spirit prays"? The answer lies in recognizing that "spirit" in this clause, as well as its parallel occurrences in verses 15 and 16 (and v. 2), refers to the Holy Spirit. Admittedly, "my Spirit" (in the sense of the Holy Spirit) is difficult, at least the initial impression it makes. Considerations in the context, however, point to this as Paul's intended meaning. A key is his immediately preceding use of "spirit" in verse 12a, translated literally: "since you are zealous of spirits." The expression "zealous of spirits," too, is an unusual one but is unquestionably a reference to the Holy Spirit, unless we take the doubtful position that Paul here reflects his view that the gifts are communicated to the church by angels or mediating spirits. The plural usage, in combination with "zealous," refers to gifts, emphasizing that they are the Spirit's gifts. The reference is to the plurality of the gifts of the Spirit in terms of the Spirit himself. This is the uniform sense of the standard English translations: "zealous of spiritual gifts" (KJV, NASB), "eager to have spiritual gifts" (NIV), "eager for gifts of the Spirit" (NEB), "eager for manifestations of the Spirit" (RSV).

A similar plural usage is present later in the chapter: "Spirits of prophets are subject to prophets" (v. 32; cf. Rev. 22:6). The thought is not that each prophet is to control his own (human) spirit. For one thing, while "spirit" is more plausibly anthropological here than in verses 14–16, that is not likely, since elsewhere in the chapter Paul associates prophecy with intelligible speech that involves the mind (v. 19; cf. 6). Rather Paul is saying that the prophetic gift given to each prophet by the Spirit is subject to the control of the prophet. "It is for prophets to control prophetic inspiration" (NEB). Again, as in verse 12, a particular gift of the Spirit is referred to in terms of the Spirit himself.

According to verse 2, "the one who speaks in a tongue . . . speaks mysteries by the Spirit." Because an anthropological spirit is excluded in verses 14 and 32, the reference here is likewise not to the human spirit, but, as is more likely on other grounds anyway, the Holy Spirit.

In verse 14, then, picking up and continuing the immediately preceding use of "spirit" (v. 12), Paul describes the gift of tongues as a particular, individual reception of the Holy Spirit himself by the speaker ("my Spirit," "the Spirit in [given to] me"). The contrast in the verse is between the Holy Spirit and the mind of the recipient, between the Spirit's activity in the gift of tongues and the inactivity of the recipient's mind. The New English Bible has captured the thought here precisely, better than other translations: "the Spirit in me prays, but my intellect lies fallow."[1]

---

1. Apart from rendering "tongues" with "ecstatic utterance," the translation of vv. 13–19 as a whole in the NEB is instructive. The broader background for the use of πνεῦμα in vv. 12, 14–16, 32, is Paul's (and the rest of the New Testament's) application of impersonal modes of expression to the Holy Spirit elsewhere: e.g., "sealing" (Eph. 1:13; 4:30); "filling" (Luke 1:15; Acts 2:4; Eph. 5:18); "quenching" (I Thess. 5:19); the Spirit as "down payment" (II Cor. 1:22; 5:5; Eph. 1:14) and "firstfruits" (Rom. 8:23).

Conclusion: What Paul says about tongues-speaking shows its fully inspired origin in the sense that the words of the speaker are the words of the Holy Spirit. His speech capacities are so taken over by the Spirit that the words spoken are not his, except in the sense that his voice is employed. Involved is a form of inspiration that even "goes beyond" the full, comprehending utilization of the human subject that is usually the case in the high inspiration of the biblical writers. In terms of the pairing of tongues with prophecy, the overall contrast of the chapter is not the Spirit-actualized expression of one side of man (his spirit, the preconceptual) in distinction from the Spirit-actualized expression of another (his mind, the conceptual), but Spirit-worked speech (the words of the Spirit) which in the one case (prophecy) does, and in the other case (tongues) does not, utilize the speaker's existing language (conceptual) capacities.

2. The inspired and thus revelatory character of tongues is confirmed by what Paul says about their *content.*
   a. A first consideration is that what the tongues-speaker articulates is capable of being *interpreted* (12:10, 30; 14:5, 13, 26–28). Leaving open here the question whether or not tongues at Corinth were existing (foreign) languages, as they were at Pentecost (Acts 2:6, 8, 11), and without entering into a linguistically adequate discussion of what constitutes language, the fact of their interpretability shows tongues to be genuine language. Whatever the precise characteristics of the tongues-phenomenon, it is language in the conventional, prevailing sense, language as a vehicle for conceptualization and the communication of intelligible meaning. As the words of the Holy Spirit, tongues are language within the scope of God's comprehensible speech to the covenant community (e.g., Heb. 1:1f.; 2:3).
   The position is sometimes taken that the gift of interpretation is a kind of intuitive, empathetic capacity by which the mind-less utterance of one member of the congregation is given intelligible meaning by another, a gift by which the preconceptual dimension in man voiced by one member is given rational, conceptual shape by another. But such a view is not only foreign to the biblical usage of "interpret" elsewhere (ἑρμηνεύω and its compounds) but

also presupposes the view of tongues we have already discussed and rejected as unbiblical.

The only reason tongues-speech is unintelligible to the listeners is that they do not understand the *language* being spoken (by the Spirit). Interpretation functions to remove that barrier to understanding. The gift of interpretation, therefore, is essentially translation (of inspired revelation), without the translation necessarily being word for word. An approximate, but helpful analogy is the way in which the Gospel writers transmit the words of Jesus, bringing them over accurately but not necessarily verbatim from one language (probably Aramaic), strange to the original readers, into another language (Greek) familiar to them. The interpretability of tongues, together with their inspired origin, shows them to be a meaningful communication (revelation) from God.

b. The inspired, revelatory character of tongues is also seen in the fact that by the Spirit "the one who speaks in a tongue . . . speaks mysteries" (14:2). Here and in the immediate context Paul is undoubtedly emphasizing that, unlike prophecy, tongues are unintelligible to others (cf. vv. 2a, 2b, 3, 4a, 5b). However, this clause does not simply make an *adverbial* statement about tongues ("the one who speaks in a tongue . . . speaks *unintelligibly, incomprehensibly*"); it also says something *substantive*, that is, something positive about the content of tongues.

Two considerations support this view. For one thing, a purely adverbial use of "mystery" is not found or supported in the considerable use that Paul makes of the term elsewhere, or in the handful of occurrences in the rest of the New Testament. Equally important is the only other occurrence of "mystery" in the context (chaps. 12–14) in 13:2 ("if I have the gift of prophecy, and know all mysteries and all knowledge . . ."). Particularly in view of the sustained comparison between prophecy and tongues which controls chapter 14 (cf. 13:1f., 8), it is difficult to deny a definite tie between 13:2 and 14:2 or to dissociate "knowing (all) mysteries" from "speaking mysteries."

Earlier, in examining prophecy, we discussed the use of "mystery" in 13:2, noting that the term is a central one in Paul's vocabulary for revelation. It emphasizes that what is revealed is inaccessible to human effort and disclosed by God unilaterally.

Consequently, "mysteries" specifies the inspired, revelatory nature of tongues as well as prophecy. Even if "mystery" were not per se a term for revelation, in 14:2 it still, by analogy with 13:2 and Paul's usage elsewhere, denotes content. In the light of the context (especially v. 14; cf. v. 2) it would still describe an intelligible, conceptual content which originates with and is expressed by the Holy Spirit in a way that does not at all involve the conceptual capacity (mind) of the tongues-speaker; in other words, it would still describe a revelation.

At the same time "mysteries" does serve, as already noted, to accent the fact that, apart from interpretation, tongues-speech is unintelligible to others. In this respect tongues are similar to the parables of Jesus (with their undoubted revelatory content). His (uninterpreted) parables serve to veil from "outsiders" "the mystery of the kingdom of God" (Mark 4:11 and parallels; see especially Matt. 13:10–17). The parables give expression to the mysteries of the kingdom in a way that conceals them from those outside the circle of Jesus' disciples. (Cf. too the tie between "kingdom" and "mystery" for Paul in I Cor. 15:50f., implicit also in Rom. 11:25f.)

I Corinthians 13:2 and 14:2 together point to what prophecy and tongues have in common: both are revelatory word-gifts. We may even speak of the essentially prophetic nature of tongues (cf. Acts 2:17f.), the difference being that tongues, unlike prophecy, require interpretation to be understood by others.

In I Corinthians 14 Paul says that "one who speaks in a tongue does not speak to men, but to God" (v. 2) and that tongues involve "praying," "singing," and "giving thanks" to God (vv. 14–17). An argument sometimes raised against the revelatory nature of tongues at Corinth is that this Godward direction of tongues is not the direction of revelation. Such an appeal, however, overlooks the Psalms and other doxological portions of Scripture. Are we to say that because they are addressed to God and not to men, they are therefore not revelation? On the contrary, with their Godward direction they are inspired revelation and recorded in Scripture in order that they may edify his covenant people, and this is precisely what (interpreted) tongues also are to do (v. 5).

Conclusion: An examination of Paul's teaching on (1) the origin and (2) the content of tongues shows that for tongues, as well as prophecy, a revelatory aspect is at the core of the gift and inseparable from it. The pairing of prophecy and tongues that structures I Corinthians 14 ultimately roots in the fact that both are *revelatory* word-gifts. The functional equivalence of prophecy and interpreted tongues extends beyond the fact that both are edifying (14:5) to the fact that they are both inspired revelation. The notion of nonrevelatory tongues, as the uninhibited vocalizing of the preconceptual, mind-less side of the personality, or in any other form, is not taught in I Corinthians 12–14, or elsewhere in the New Testament for that matter.

3. Before concluding this section on tongues, some related issues may be discussed briefly.

a. One frequently debated question concerns the specific language phenomenon of the tongues at Corinth. Tongues at Pentecost are clearly existing languages; the point is made repeatedly that they are native to their hearers (Acts 2:6, 8, 11). But what about Corinth? Are tongues there also existing languages or an unknown, perhaps heavenly, language? (They must be genuine language of some kind; some type of linguistically-unstructured, preconceptual vocalization, whether or not "ecstatic," is excluded for reasons already noted, e.g., interpretability.)

The answer to this question is not as crucial to New Testament teaching on tongues as is usually supposed. We confine ourselves here to a couple of comments which point to the conclusion that the phenomenon at Corinth and Pentecost is the same, that is, existing languages. For one thing, it should be recognized that nothing in I Corinthians 12–14 decisively excludes the phenomenon at Corinth from being known, existing languages; nothing there *demands* that the tongues are some new, previously unspoken (heavenly?) language(s). Note that 14:23 ("will they not say that you are out of your mind?" NIV) cannot be appealed to, because it describes a reaction much like that of one part of the crowd at Pentecost (Acts 2:13: "They have had too much wine"; cf. v. 15).

Further, in Acts we find indications of a definite association between prophecy and tongues, indications of the same pairing of the two present in I Corinthians. This at least suggests that the phenomenon in each case is the same. The conclusion to Luke's account of Paul's encounter with the disciples at Ephesus is that after the Holy Spirit came upon the latter, "they were speaking in tongues and prophesying" (Acts 19:6). This appears to parallel the description of what took place among the Gentiles: after the Holy Spirit fell upon them, they were "speaking in tongues and magnifying God" (10:46; cf. v. 44). This apparent interchange of "prophesying" with "magnifying God" ("acclaiming the greatness of God," NEB) points back to Pentecost, where tongues-speaking itself is "declaring the great things of God" (2:11). The assumption here is that tongues are the same language phenomenon in chapters 10 and 19 that they are in chapter 2, an assumption warranted, at least for chapter 10, by 11:15 ("just as upon us at the beginning"; cf. 10:45). Acts, then, displays an association between prophecy and tongues like that found in Paul. This suggests that the language phenomenon in each instance is of the same kind (known human languages).

b. Not only does Acts closely associate prophecy and tongues. In chapter 2 tongues *are* prophecy. This is clear from Peter's sermon where tongues, as the fulfillment of Joel's prophecy (Joel 2:28–32), are within the scope of "your sons and daughters will prophesy" (v. 17), a point emphasized by Peter's interpretive gloss on the Joel-citation at the end of verse 18: "and they shall prophesy" (cf. also the indication of the prophetic nature of tongues in v. 11, noted in the preceding paragraph). This ties in with what has emerged repeatedly in our discussion of I Corinthians 14, namely, the functional equivalence of prophecy and interpreted tongues, and permits the generalization that New Testament tongues are a form of prophecy. Tongues are a mode of prophecy, if the latter is taken in a slightly expanded but essentially unchanged sense.

c. What about the private, devotional use of tongues? In I Corinthians 14 Paul is primarily concerned with the public use of tongues when the church assembles. At the same time the passage does apparently contain indications which point to some kind of private exercise of the gift (vv. 18f., less clearly 4 and 28). Such indications, however, hardly support the (in some cases even consuming) preoccupation with a private, devotional use of tongues often advocated, largely by appeal to this passage. In any case, such private uses of tongues as may be contemplated by Paul would be controlled by the following considerations:

(1) Any private use of tongues is *not* a gift somehow separable from, in addition to, or independent of its public exercise together with interpretation, as if the gift of tongues is given to some for private use, to others for public use (with interpretation). Rather, any private use of tongues is a strictly ancillary, peripheral aspect of the gift; private tongues are an accompanying, subsidiary benefit enjoyed by the recipient of the gift (to be interpreted) with its distinctive revelatory function. Note that it is just the prayer-tongue and the praise (song)-tongue (vv. 14f.), usually seen to be central to the private exercise of the gift, which stand under the repetition of Paul's command for interpretation (v. 13; cf. v. 5). The view which holds that tongues are given primarily for the personal prayer life of the believer and not for public exercise in the congregation, along with interpretation, can be said only to have completely inverted Paul's outlook in I Corinthians 14.

An instructive parallel at this point, including the "self-edifying" value of tongues (v. 4), is Paul's own experience touched on in II Corinthians 12:1ff. In verses 2-4 he recalls certain sublime and memorable events: "caught up to the third heaven [to Paradise]," "heard inexpressible words which man may not speak." Although he prefers not to "boast" about them (vv. 1, 5, 6), he is compelled to do so by the necessity in the larger context (chaps. 10–13) of having to defend his apostolic office and the gospel he preaches. The point to consider, keeping this context in mind, is that these experiences are not an end in themselves, or merely for Paul's private benefit; they are an integral, yet subordinate feature of the visions and "surpassingly great" revelations (vv. 1, 7) which lie at the base of his (apostolic) gospel preached to the (whole) church (cf. Gal. 1:11–17). These events, though of an intensely personal character, do not fall within some private sector of personal religious experience, distinct from his apostolic ministry, but are rather, as the larger context makes plain, an attendant aspect of that *ministry*. This provides a perspective essential for understanding both Paul's statement that he speaks in tongues more than all (I Cor. 14:18) and his wish that all might speak in tongues (v. 5). Any private use of tongues attaches to the one gift given to be exercised publicly for the edification of the congregation as a whole.

(2) Another consideration that controls any private use of tongues is the principle of differential distribution. The gift of tongues, including its private exercise, is not an exception to the principle that no one gift is intended for everyone in the church. Consequently, the view that the *public* use of tongues (with interpretation) is given only to *some* in the church, while their *private* use, without interpretation, is (ideally) for *all*, puts a strain on statements like I Corinthians 14:5, 18, 23 beyond what they can bear ("I wish that you all spoke in tongues"; "I speak in tongues more than you all"; "If . . . all speak in tongues . . . ").

The "all" in these statements is hypothetical, and surely to be understood in the light of the negative answer required by the rhetorical question of 12:30: "All do not speak with tongues, do they?" (NASB). This "no, they don't," it should be stressed again, does not trace back to some debilitating factor in the church (e.g., lack of faith, failure to seek the gift), but is rooted in the edifying reality of the Spirit's differential distribution (v. 11), which takes shape as the harmony among the diversity of gifts and functions variously distributed among the many parts of the one body. (Note, too, that although in the comparable statement in 7:7 Paul writes with reference to his own unmarried state, "I wish that all were like I myself am," the rest of the verse ["but each has his own gift from God . . . "] and the chapter as a whole make plain that the statement is hypothetical and does not express a norm, or even an ideal, for that matter.)

According to Romans 8:26 and 27, "the Spirit helps us in our weakness; for we do not know what to pray for as we ought, but the Spirit himself intercedes for us with groans that words cannot express. And he who searches our hearts knows the mind of the Spirit, because the Spirit intercedes for the saints in accordance with God's will." The effort is often made to connect this passage directly with I Corinthians 14, particularly praying in tongues. However, that Paul is not describing tongues here is plain for two reasons: (a) The Spirit's intercessory activity described in these verses is for every believer ("the saints") and a reality in each without exception; the gift of tongues is not for every believer (I Cor. 12:30). (b) Tongues are capable of being interpreted and can be made understandable in existing languages (I Cor. 14:5, 13); the Spirit's intercessory groans are "inexpressible," they cannot be put into words, and only God who searches the hearts knows the Spirit's meaning ("mind").

These verses, however, are relevant to issues often raised in discussing tongues, and that fact needs to be appreciated. Paul describes the Spirit's help to us in our weakness. In the immediate context of Romans 8 this "weakness" has the broadest conceivable scope; it includes but is not limited to particular struggles and difficulties peculiar to one believer in distinction from others. Rather it is the weakness-"sufferings" of "the present time" (v. 18). This time is "this present evil age" (Gal. 1:4), which in its sinful corruption and futility (Rom. 8:20) continues to unfold until its final destruction at Christ's return (I Cor. 15:23–28), destruction made certain because it has actually already dawned in the final salvation of "the age-to-come," which is revealed in his sufferings and glorification (cf. Rom. 8:17) and experienced in its "firstfruits" by believers (v. 23). It is the time of "groaning," in which believers, with the whole creation in anxious expectation, eagerly await their being openly revealed as the sons of God, their adoption as sons in the redemption (resurrection) of their bodies (vv. 19–23). All told, "weakness" is the mode of the believer's entire existence in "this present evil age" with all the limitations, suffering, and temptation to sin this existence involves (cf. Heb. 4:15). "The present time" is a time of weakness.

Romans 8:26 particularizes this comprehensive weakness and brings it to a focus in the matter of prayer. Scripture clearly indicates what believers are to pray for and how they are to pray (e.g., the Lord's Prayer, Matt. 6:9–13), and yet "we do not know what to pray for as we ought." The veil of our limitations—our ignorance, our shortsightedness, our uncertainty, our lack of concentration, our sinful doubts and confusion—constantly casts a shadow over our prayers, keeping them from being as they ought to be, fully "according to the will of God" (v. 27), "according to his purpose" (v. 28). Positively, in our "best" moments, when we are overwhelmed with the glory of God, the grandeur of his salvation, and the wonder of his love, we experience the weakness-inadequacy of our praise and thanksgiving.

But the ministry of the Spirit, Paul says, is adequate to this massive need of believers; he helps them as this pervasive weakness inevitably affects their prayers. To the groaning of creation in travail (v. 22) and the inward groans of believers themselves in their mortality (v. 23) are joined the Spirit's own groans in believers (not the Spirit present and at work in our groans; not what we do but what he does). He is involved in our weakness yet at the same time transcends it. The intercessory groans of the Spirit are "inexpressible" or "wordless," not because they are without meaning, but because they are beyond our capacities as creatures. We are not able to comprehend them or express them. These groanings take place in the believer but are not understood (or perceived) by him. Only God, the searcher of hearts, understands them. He alone knows (and acknowledges) the absolute efficacy of this intercession rendered there (in our hearts) for us in perfect accordance with his will.

This passage reminds believers of their weakness, which is pervasive and inescapable as long as "this present time" continues, and comforts them with the knowledge of the Spirit's help to them in this weakness. The "secret" of effective prayer is not the gift of tongues understood as the Spirit's activity in some believers which briefly suspends their weakness by momentarily removing the inhibiting barriers of language and providing new capacities for self-expression in prayer. Rather what makes prayer efficacious is the intercessory groaning of the Spirit in all believers, coupled with the intercession of the exalted Christ on their behalf (v. 34). This intercession does not produce fleeting moments of temporary isolation from our weakness, moments constantly needing to be recaptured, but because it is constant and perfect, it constantly and perfectly sustains us in our prayers with all their flaws, as long as we continue in this present time of our weakness.

d. A widespread view is that tongues are given for the decisive transformation and renewal of lives, that the gift brings to its recipient, among other things, deeper devotion to Christ, greater fervency and freedom in prayer, and a more intense desire to witness. But where does the New Testament teach that this is the purpose of tongues? To raise this question is not to deny or be ungrateful for the renewal that may be evident in the lives of those who claim they have received the gift of tongues. But surely the overall thrust of I Corinthians 12–14 is in precisely the *opposite* direction, especially in the specific case of *tongues*. The "hymn to love" in chapter 13 is not a parenthetical insertion which could have been omitted without really effecting the flow of Paul's argument; it is essential to his argument. His sustained point is that those qualities which are to characterize every believer, such as love for God and neighbor (and the rest of the Spirit's "fruit," cf. Gal. 5:22f.), are *not* dependent upon receiving any one of the gifts mentioned in chapter 12. And especially in the light of what he goes on to say in chapter 14, it is clear that he particularly has tongues in mind.

From this we are bound to draw this conclusion concerning the individual reception of spiritual gifts: no one of the gifts variously distributed in the church, including tongues, is necessary for the worship and witness God is seeking in each one of his people. No gift, including tongues, is integral to true spirituality. The gifts of the Spirit are not "means of grace" indispensable, like God's Word, the sacraments, and prayer, for personal sanctification and growth in grace. In giving gifts to his church God does not place some of his people at a disadvantage in relation to others with reference to "the holiness without which no one will see the Lord" (Heb. 12:14).

V

The Question of Cessation

The view is widely held today that all the gifts mentioned in Romans 12, I Corinthians 12, and Ephesians 4 were given to continue in the church until Christ's return. The view that certain gifts have ceased is seen as a desperate ploy in flagrant disregard of plain biblical teaching, a lame, after-the-fact rationalization of a church embarrassed by the absence of these gifts in its midst. Nevertheless, there are several lines of New Testament teaching that in their convergence point to the conclusion that prophecy and tongues were intended to cease prior to Christ's return and have in fact ceased. In this chapter, these lines will be sketched, some of them more fully than others.

A. The Temporary Nature of the Apostolate

Passing over the details of rather involved debate among biblical scholars over the role of the apostle, it is a fair generalization to say that in the New Testament the term has one of two basic references: (1) It can refer to the representative of a particular church, temporarily delegated for a specific task (II Cor. 8:23; Phil. 2:25; perhaps Acts 14:4, 14). (2) The more important and dominant reference, as in I Corinthians 12:28, 29 and Ephesians 4:11, is to the apostles of Christ. In this latter sense the apostles are limited in number (just how many may remain an open question here), and confined to the first generation of the church's history. This temporary character of the apostolate can be seen from several angles: (1) One requirement is that the apostle be an eye-and-ear witness of the resurrected Christ (John 15:27; Acts 1:8, 22; 10:41). Paul sees this requirement as having been met in his case by Christ's appearance to him on the Damascus road (I Cor. 9:1; 15:8f.; cf. Acts 9:3–8; 22:6–11; 26:12–18). (2) Paul suggests that he is the last of the apostles (I Cor. 15:8f.: " . . . last of all, . . . the least of the apostles . . . "; perhaps also 4:9: " . . . us apostles last of all," where, most likely, "us" does not include Apollos [v. 6] but is limited to Paul, since the experiences attributed to "us" in the immediately following verses [9b–13] are best understood as Paul's own individual experience). (3) The Pastoral Epistles make plain that Paul views Timothy as much as anyone else as his personal successor. The task of gospel ministry laid down by Paul is to be taken up and continued by Timothy (and others). Yet Paul never designates him an apostle. According to the New Testament, "apostolic succession" in a personal sense is a contradiction in terms. The activity of the apostles in the church is "once for all." Anyone working with the New Testament, then, is bound to recognize the temporary character of the apostolate. This conclusion has been denied down through the history of the church and still has those today who resist it. With them we must regretfully part company at this point. But where it is accepted, several other conclusions are involved. For one thing, since, with all that is unique and preeminent about the office of apostle, Paul nonetheless lists it as one (the first) among other gifts given to the church (I Cor. 12:28f.; Eph. 4:11), it is plainly not the case that *all* the gifts mentioned by Paul are to continue until Christ's return. Nor, then, does the position that one (or more) of these gifts has been withdrawn, necessarily deny the authority and continuing applicability of Scripture. Further, the distinction, *apostolic-postapostolic* is not imposed on the New Testament and church history, but is given by the New Testament itself. The Pastoral Epistles, in particular, are written to make provision for the postapostolic future of the church. Consequently, the demand incumbent on all who recognize the temporary nature of the apostolate, especially in view of its obvious and central importance, is to determine what elements of the church's life described in the New Testament are so integrally associated with the ministry of the apostles that they disappear along with the withdrawal of the apostolate, and what elements continue on into the postapostolic period of the church.

B. The Foundational Character of the Apostolic Witness

The single most important activity of the apostles is surely that, already intimated, of *witness* to Christ (e.g., John 15:27; Acts 1:8; 13:31). The apostles bear witness, authorized and empowered by Christ himself, to his resurrection as the fulfillment of covenant history (e.g., Luke 24:48; Acts 1:22; 2:32; 4:33; 10:39–41). Because of the centrality and the far-reaching implications of Christ's death and resurrection, this witness is a comprehensive interpretation of his person and work. It is not confined to the proclamation of the basic facts of the gospel to unbelievers. Rather, it is of one piece with, better, it is the totality of apostolic preaching and teaching, whether oral or written (II Thess. 2:15). It consists in declaring nothing less than "the whole counsel of God" (Acts 20:27), disclosed in the coming of the kingdom of God (e.g., v. 25) and the revelation of the mystery in Christ (e.g., Rom. 16:25f.), for the salvation of his people and the renewal of the entire creation (II Cor. 5:17; Rev. 21:5).

Perhaps the most sweeping perspective on this task of witness is provided by Ephesians 2:19ff. There Paul views the new covenant church (cf. vv. 11ff.) as the result of God's great housebuilding activity in the period between the resurrection and return of Christ (cf. I Peter 2:4–8). In so doing Paul calls the apostles, along with Christ as the cornerstone, the foundation of the church-house (v. 20). This is not said in order to shade or deny the finality of Christ's person and work as the sole foundation of the church (I Cor. 3:11), but to include the apostles and their activity in a specific respect. The apostles do supplement Christ's work, not by additional atoning, redemptive labors of their own, but by bearing witness to that work. In the terms of this passage, the apostles are not, as Christ is, the peace who has made the Jews and Gentiles one by destroying the enmity and reconciling both to God, and so to each other (vv. 14–16). But they are the spokesmen by whom the exalted Christ has come and preached peace-unity to both Jew and Gentile (v. 17). To the once-for-all, foundational work of Christ, consummated in his death and resurrection, is joined the once-for-all, foundational witness of the apostles to that work. Such witness is anticipated in Matthew 16:18, where Jesus calls confessing Peter (cf. v. 16), as representative of the other apostles, the rock on which he will build his church.

The apostles are not part of the foundation because of their chronological priority in the church (if so, Paul's inclusion would be doubtful; cf. especially I Cor. 15:8f.), or because their number is fixed (the New Testament is not concerned to delimit their precise number). Nor are they the foundation because of their (Jewish) race. The point of the passage is not the unity of Jew and Gentile exhibited in the fact that the Gentiles are built upon a Jewish foundation, but the unity of Jew and Gentile because both have been built upon the cornerstone, Christ, who, together with the apostles and prophets, makes up one foundation. The apostles are not part of the foundation for any reason or characteristic of their persons apart from the exercise of their (apostolic) functions. On the other hand, the foundation is not the apostolic witness in abstraction from the apostles themselves. The choice between a personal and impersonal understanding of the foundation is a false dilemma exegetically. The foundation is the apostles as *witnessing* apostles, the apostles in terms of the revelation given to them and spoken by them (cf. Eph. 3:5).

It is also important to grasp that the foundation here is absolute and historical in character. It does not describe particular situations which the gospel reaches for the first time, regardless of time and place. Rather, it is part of a single, comprehensive redemptive-historical image (house-building) which pictures, in the case of the apostles as well as Christ, what is done once, at the beginning of the church's history, and does not bear repeating. The period beyond this foundational period is not a time of perpetually relaying the foundation but is the superstructure built upon that (definitively laid) foundation.

The foundational nature of the apostles' comprehensive witness enables us to appreciate a correlate emphasis on the apostolic "tradition" to be held fast, found already in II Thessalonians (2:15; 3:6), on the "deposit" to be kept, in the Pastorals (I Tim. 6:20; II Tim. 1:14), and on the "faith once for all delivered to the saints" (Jude 3). This emphasis reflects the binding authority of the apostles' witness and establishes lines that prepare for and point the way to the eventual emergence of the New Testament canon (see II Peter 3:16, where Paul's letters are already seen on the same level as "the other Scriptures").

C. The Foundational Character of Prophecy

Ephesians 2:20 associates "prophets" with the apostles in the activity of foundational witness or word ministry. The identity of these prophets has been a matter of some dispute. One still popular understanding is that they are the Old Testament prophets. "Apostles and prophets," then, is one way of indicating the unity of the old and new covenants and that the church is based on both. However, a reference to Old Testament prophets is unlikely in view of (1) the word order ("prophets," not "apostles," would naturally stand first if Old Testament prophets were intended) and (2) the immediate context, which is intent on stressing the newness of the new covenant, with the inclusion of the Gentiles as well as the Jews in Christ's body; it is excluded by (3) the occurrence of the same combination (apostles and prophets) only a few verses later in 3:5, where the prophets are plainly part of the present life of the church ("now") in contrast to the old covenant era ("which was not made known to men in other generations as it has now been revealed by the Spirit to God's holy apostles and prophets").

Another position sometimes taken is that "prophets" (in 3:5 as well as 2:20) describes the apostles ("the apostles who are also prophets"). This is possible grammatically and the apostles do exercise prophetic functions (e.g., Rom. 11:25f.; I Cor. 15:51ff.; I Thess. 4:15ff.; cf. I Cor. 14:6). Probably there is nothing that absolutely excludes this view.

A combination of considerations, however, is decisively against it. To begin with, in Ephesians 4:11, where Paul lists some of the gifts of the exalted Christ to the church (vv. 7ff.), the apostles as a group are plainly distinguished from the prophets as a group ("He gave some to be apostles, some to be prophets, some to be evangelists . . . "). Inasmuch as this verse is part of the same larger unit (2:11—4:16) in which Paul is discussing the whole church and its composition as the "new creation" body of Christ, it is highly unlikely that without any explanation he would use "prophets" in two different senses. Ephesians 4:7–16 advances Paul's description of the church by pointing out the harmony of the different gifts given by Christ to the body. Most likely, then, 4:11 shows that the prophets mentioned earlier in 2:20 and 3:5 are along with the apostles, but distinct from them, one among the gifts of the exalted Christ. It is not likely that the "apostles and prophets," who are mentioned as the foundation of the church, are other than the "apostles" and "prophets," who serve its "upbuilding" (4:12). In fact, in view of the larger context, their foundational (witnessing) function is their specific contribution to the larger, more general picture of edification in 4:11–16.

This set of observations is enforced by several others. In I Corinthians 12:28, the only other place where Paul mentions apostles and prophets together, he clearly distinguishes them as separate groups ("And in the church God has appointed first of all apostles, second prophets, third teachers . . ."; see also the distinction made in Rev. 18:20). Moreover, this verse is in a context quite similar to Ephesians 2–4; in I Corinthians 12 Paul is concerned in a comprehensive way with the structure of the church (Christ's body) as made up of Jews and Gentiles (v. 13), and gifted for service.

Also, if Paul were intending to identify the apostles as prophets in Ephesians 2:20 and 3:5, then some explanation of this usage to his readers would have been necessary. It is true, as we noted earlier in chapter III, that the line between certain gifts is not a hard and fast one, and that, in particular, apostles exercise the functions of prophets and teachers. Paul as an individual apostle calls himself a preacher and teacher (I Tim. 2:7; II Tim. 1:11). But he never calls himself or any of the other apostles a prophet. More decisive is the *plural* usage in 2:20 and 3:5. The apostles are in view as a group. Elsewhere Paul never designates the apostles as prophets or teachers or in terms of any of the other distinct ministries in the church. To do so would have been confusing. To be sure, the activity of prophesying was not rigidly confined to one group in the church; the gift could be given temporarily on particular occasions to those who were not prophets (cf. Acts 19:6). But that is just the point. The usage in Acts and Revelation as well as Paul makes plain that "prophets" designates those who in their frequent or regular exercise of the gift of prophecy are a distinct group within the church, distinguished also from the apostles, who likewise exercise prophetic functions. For Paul to have used "prophets" in Ephesians 2:20 and 3:5 other than in this sense familiar to his readers would have been lost on them without at least some word of explanation, especially since he goes on in the same context (4:11) to reinforce the conventional usage of the word.

For these reasons, then, we ought to conclude, as do the great majority of commentators, that Ephesians 2:20 and 3:5 refer to the New Testament prophets in distinction from the apostles. Once this is grasped then the lack of the (repeated) definite article before "prophets" in both instances shows how closely Paul associates them with the apostles as a unit in the activity of foundational, revelatory witness to Christ and the "mystery" revealed in him.

The objection that revelation concerning this mystery is not the "kind" of revelation given to the prophets rests on a misunderstanding of the total New Testament teaching on prophecy (see chap. IV, section B) and a too restricted understanding of the mystery. The specific case of Agabus (Acts 11:28; 21:10f.), as I will presently try to show, is evidence for, not against, the foundational character of prophecy. The inclusion of the Gentiles in the church, stressed in this passage (cf. especially 3:6ff.), is a prominent aspect of the mystery, but only an aspect. The mystery is nothing less than Christ himself in all his saving fulness (Col. 2:2f.), the gospel in all its aspects (Eph. 6:19; cf. Rom. 16:25f.).

Consequently, a major conclusion in our study from Ephesians 2:20 is that the New Testament prophets, along with the apostles, are the foundation of the church. They have a foundational, that is, temporary, noncontinuing function in the church's history, and so by God's design pass out of its life, along with the apostles. The following observations bear on this conclusion and efforts to resist it:

1. As a general guideline for interpretation, the decisive, controlling significance of Ephesians 2:20 (in its context) needs to be appreciated. It and the other passages that bear on prophecy, like I Corinthians 14, are not of the same order of magnitude exegetically. I Corinthians 14, for instance, may well reflect circumstances in other churches; but in most of its considerable detail it has a relatively narrow focus and is confined to the particular situation at Corinth. Ephesians, on the other hand, may well be a circular letter, originally intended by Paul for a wider audience than the congregation at Ephesus. More importantly, 2:20 is part of a section that surveys the church as a whole in a most sweeping and comprehensive fashion. Ephesians 2:20 stands back, views the whole building, and notes the place of prophecy in it (as part of the foundation); I Corinthians 14 and the other passages on prophecy examine one of the parts from within.

Ephesians 2:20, then, with its broad scope ought to have a pivotal and governing role in seeking to understand other New Testament statements on prophecy with a narrower, more particular and detailed focus, especially since, as we saw above (chap. IV, section B), the various statements of the New Testament on prophecy all refer to a common phenomenon (with various aspects). Ephesians 2:20 makes a generalization that covers all the other New Testament statements on prophecy.

2. A frequent objection to our conclusion that prophecy, along with the apostles, has been withdrawn from the church takes the form of a counterposition. This is the view that prophets as bearers of foundational revelation have indeed been taken from the church, but that in addition to and more or less parallel with this foundational function of prophecy, which has ceased, there are other functions, in view, for instance, in I Corinthians 14, which are intended to continue and are in fact present in the church today.

One response to this viewpoint must be to reemphasize what was just said about Ephesians 2:20 and its exegetical "weight": it makes a generalization about prophecy that covers *all* its functions and says that they have ceased. Further, granting the fully revelatory character of prophecy (discussed above in chap. IV, section B), such a view inevitably involves a dualistic understanding of revelation. In one form or other, it distinguishes between canonical revelation for the whole church and private revelations for individual believers or groups of believers, between a collective, inscripturated revelation of what is "necessary for salvation" and revelations that "go beyond" the Bible and bear on individual life situations, needs, and concerns.

Such an understanding of revelation is in irreconcilable conflict with what the Bible itself shows to be the covenantal, redemptive-historical character of *all* revelation. God does not reveal himself along two tracks, one public and one private. As long as revelation is viewed in the first place as God's Word to me as an individual and as given primarily to provide me with specific, explicit directives and answers to the particular concerns and perplexities of my individual life situation, it is fundamentally misunderstood and a sense of the inadequacy of the Bible alone as a guide for life is almost inevitable.

According to the overall witness of Scripture, at least two characteristics are basic to all revelation and control the giving of it. Very briefly, (a) revelation is *covenantal*. God reveals himself as the God of the covenant. He reveals himself, not to a mass of undifferentiated individuals, but to his covenant people, in order to build them up and make their number complete as one people. His revelation is always to and in the interests of the whole covenant people, although the exact bearing of any revelation may vary from individual to individual, depending on their differing life situations. (b) Revelation is *redemptive-historical*. Apart from the brief period before the fall, God reveals himself as the Redeemer of his covenant people and the Savior of the world. Revelation is given as a component part of God's work in history to accomplish, once for all, the salvation of his covenant people. Revelation is an integral element in the ongoing covenant history which has reached its initial consummation in the sufferings, death, and exaltation of Christ. It documents this history, particularly Christ as the fulfillment of the promises, and interprets it by drawing out the implications for the life and obedience of the redeemed covenant people. Since the history of redemption has been *definitively accomplished* and since after Pentecost its ongoing movement is delayed until Christ's return for the *application* of redemption and the ingathering of the nations to share in the salvation of the covenant, the basis and rationale for new revelations is lacking and revelation has therefore ceased.

Revelation, then, is covenantal and redemptive-historical. To be sure, Scripture gives numerous examples where revelation is addressed in a pointedly personal way to specific individuals. And it most assuredly bears on our individual life situations and concerns; it is "a lamp to *my* feet and a light to *my* path" (Ps. 119:105). But it is that only as it is the revelation given with the unfolding of covenant history to its consummation in Christ in the "fulness of time" (Gal. 4:4), the revelation spoken to the fathers by the prophets, and consummately, finally ("in these last days"), to us by the Son together with the apostles and others ("those who heard him," Heb. 1:1f.; 2:3). Revelation is the authority and guide for our lives only as and nothing less than "all things," "all the truth," revealed to the apostles and others with them on our behalf (John 14:26; 15:15; 16:13), "things," "truth," by the way, which are the things of Christ (16:14), the truth that he is (14:6), as the final Word of God (1:1), spoken once for all.

Further, salvation, the concern of covenant revelation, is not restricted to some aspect of life, nor even to the core of our existence. Rather, it is comprehensive. Nothing about us and our lives as Christians falls outside the scope of salvation in Christ. We are constantly and in all its aspects to "work out our salvation" (Phil. 2:12), according to the canonical Word God has given to his covenant people definitively, once for all, in conjunction with his definitive, once-for-all salvation. There is no room in the life of the Christian for revelation that is not concerned with or goes "beyond" what is necessary for salvation in its covenantal fulness.

Scripture leaves no place for privatized, localized revelations for specific individual needs and circumstances. The appeal to the prophecies of Agabus to support such a notion is particularly inappropriate. Their covenantal-historical character seems apparent. In the one instance (Acts 11:28), prophecy is directed toward cementing the newly-established, foundational bond of fellowship within the church between Jew and Gentile. Prophecy functions to induce the Greeks at Antioch (v. 27; cf. v. 20) to contribute famine relief for their (Jewish) brothers in Judea (vv. 29f.). In other words, this prophecy is directly related to an important aspect of the mystery revealed in Christ (cf. Eph. 3:6). In the other instance (Acts 21:10f.), prophecy concerns the unfolding of Paul's apostolic ministry to the Gentiles (cf. 20:23). Along more general lines, the subject matter of prophecy is "mysteries" (I Cor. 13:2), always a redemptive-historical category in Paul.

3. Closely related to the point just discussed is the relationship between prophecy and the New Testament canon. It will not do to reject this question as irrelevant, a "red herring" which confuses the issue. The foundational, apostolic era of the church is as such (foundational) an "open canon" period, that is, a period in which material for the (eventually consolidated) new covenant canon is in the process of formation. Prophecy is one of the principal revelatory word-gifts operative in this period. It is a foundational word-gift in two distinct respects: (a) in producing what is eventually recognized to be canonical (e.g., the Book of Revelation); but also, and primarily, (b) in meeting contemporary needs in the church that are bound up with and peculiar to the foundational, that is, incomplete canon situation. The same distinction applies to the ministry of the apostles. While several, notably Paul, are prominent in producing (inscripturated) revelation that permanently serves the church (as part of the new canon), the majority, along with the prophets, bring revelations that are intended only for the church in their own (foundational) time. In this connection, two remarks need to be made.

a. It is important to recognize that the canon and inspired, authoritative revelation, even when inscripturated, are not identical. Inspiration is a necessary, but not a sufficient condition of canonicity. Paul, for instance, refers to a previous letter from him to the Corinthians and the command it contained (I Cor. 5:9), and directs that his letter to the Colossians be exchanged with his letter presumably addressed to Laodicea, for public reading in the church (Col. 4:16; Phil. 3:1 may likewise refer to a previous letter to the Philippians). These no longer extant letters are put on a par with the canonical letters. The former are viewed as having for their readers the same inspired, revelatory authority as the latter. This shows that at the time of the apostles the circle of (authoritative) revelation was wider than what was finally included in the canon. It also shows the speciousness of the argument that the revelations through the prophets mentioned in Corinthians, just because they were not included in the canon, therefore lacked the full authority of the Word of God (spoken and written by the apostles). The overall picture is the replacement of one situation by another: at first, the church's new "canon" is the organism of God's Word being spoken and written by the apostles and prophets (in addition to the Old Testament), and then, beyond the time of the apostles, the finalized, completed organism of the collection of twenty-seven books.

   b. It is also important to appreciate that the church in its foundational period of the apostles and prophets did not possess a "sufficient" Scripture. This was especially so with reference to the momentous implications of the salvation just revealed in Christ for the church's practice and lifestyle. A comparison with the church today in this respect is instructive. At the time, say, Paul wrote I Corinthians his readers did not have access, for example, to all four Gospels with the rich, synoptically interacting perspectives they provide on Jesus' ministry and Christian discipleship, nor to the instructive outlook on the church's history in Acts, nor to Romans with its masterful statement of the gospel, nor to the prison epistles, or Hebrews, or Revelation. We must ask ourselves whether we grasp our profound advantage in the access granted us to God's completed statement of his Word.

   At any rate, for prophecy, correctly conceived of, to continue on into subsequent generations of the church, beyond its foundational period, would necessarily create tensions with the closed, finished character of the canon. In fact, such a continuation would exclude a completed canon in the strict sense. At the most, there would be room for a unit, complete in the sense of having its own relative integrity, but constantly supplemented by new, additional revelations, a notion, we have tried to show, that conflicts with the covenantal nature of all revelation, taught in Scripture.

4. Ephesians 2:20, in closely associating the prophets with the apostles, points up the need for a certain flexibility or balance in our conception of the apostles and their role. On the one hand, the apostles are "super-gifted," apparently exercising many of, perhaps all, the gifts listed in Romans 12, I Corinthians 12, and Ephesians 4. The foundational period of the church is by way of preeminence properly termed the "apostolic age." On the other hand, others, like the prophets, are associated with the apostles and share in one or more of the gifts.

On balance, the overall picture seems to be that the apostolate is the immediate nucleus or source in the church of the gifts given by the exalted Christ in this period. Certain apparently more striking or spectacular gifts (like tongues?) are called "the signs of an apostle" (II Cor. 12:12), and the gifts of the Holy Spirit distributed by God according to his will have their place as part of his corroborating witness joined to the (apostles') ear-witness ("those who heard") to salvation in Christ (Heb. 2:3f.). Yet every one of the gifts, except apostleship, is exercised by others who are not apostles. The reason the gifts can be called apostolic and yet be present in others is that the presence of these gifts in others so thoroughly depends upon and flows out of the presence in the church of the (living, functioning) apostolate.

In making this point, however, too formal or mechanical a tie between the apostles and certain gifts ought not be maintained, as if others received these gifts only at the specific direction of an apostle or by the laying on of apostolic hands. The New Testament evidence does not warrant such a conclusion, although it must be admitted that in Acts, at least, every instance of conferring sign-gifts takes place with the personal presence or oversight of apostles (2; 8:14–19; 10:44ff.; 19:6). The situation is rather the organic distribution of gifts throughout the whole body by the exalted

Christ, in view of the presence of the apostles, who among those within the body are first and central to the church's existence in this foundational era.

D. The Cessation of Tongues

We are now in a position to draw a conclusion concerning the cessation of tongues. As I have tried to show (chap. IV, section C), tongues in the New Testament are always closely associated with prophecy and, when interpreted, are functionally equivalent to prophecy, as revelation from God which edifies others. In fact, tongues are a mode of prophecy. Tongues, too, are for the foundation of the church. Accordingly, tongues are withdrawn from the life of the church along with prophecy and whatever other foundational gifts are bound up with the presence of the apostolate in the church.

This conclusion follows along the lines laid down in the preceding points of this chapter. It is not offset by evidence from church history in the centuries which immediately follow the time of the New Testament. Any evidence available from before the fourth century, such as Mark 16:17 (most likely a secondary reading) and Irenaeus, *Against Heresies* V. vi. 1, is too isolated and obscure to be decisive. Further, it is not possible exegetically, any more than for prophecy, to split the functions of tongues into those that cease and those that continue beyond the time of the apostles. The issue of the canon and its completeness, already raised with reference to prophecy, inevitably comes up in connection with tongues and their continuation.

I Corinthians 14:20–25, largely passed over so far in our discussion, may be examined here for its bearing on the conclusion that tongues have ceased.

> [20]Brothers, stop thinking like children. In regard to evil be infants, but in your thinking be adults. [21]In the Law it is written: "Through men of strange tongues and through the lips of foreigners I will speak to this people, but even then they will not listen to me," says the Lord. [22]Tongues, then, are a sign, not for believers but for unbelievers; prophecy, however, is for believ-

ers, not for unbelievers. [23]So if the whole church comes together
and everyone speaks in tongues, and some who do not understand or some unbelievers come in, will they not say that you are
out of your mind? [24]But if an unbeliever or someone who does
not understand comes in while everybody is prophesying, he
will be convinced by all that he is a sinner and will be judged by
all, [25]and the secrets of his heart will be laid bare. So he will fall
down and worship God, exclaiming, "God is really among you!"
(NIV)

These verses contain a number of difficulties and, not surpris-
ingly, have received widely diverging interpretations down
through the church's history. Even today there is no consensus on
Paul's precise train of thought in them. One major problem is
Paul's use of the Old Testament (Isa. 28:11, 12b) in verse 21. The
quotation varies from both the (Masoretic) Hebrew text and the
(Septuagint) Greek translation of the Old Testament most often
used by the New Testament writers (both of which, in turn, differ
from each other at this point). This could be either because Paul is
quoting from a different, no longer extant text, or because he gives
his own interpretive rendering.

A further difficulty concerns Paul's understanding of the verses
quoted. In its context Isaiah 28:11 is most plausibly understood as
prophesying the strange and alien speech to be heard in Judah
because of their persistent refusal to listen to the prophets' clear
gospel message of rest to the weary, summarized and recalled in
verse 12a. Usually this prophecy is seen to have had its immediate
fulfillment in the language of foreign (Assyrian and Babylonian)
invaders and occupiers, who were the instrument of God's judgment on Judah for its apostasy (cf. Isa. 33:19; Jer. 5:15) and fulfilled the covenant curse pronounced in Deuteronomy 28:49. Paul,
however, seems to imply that the message of rest in verse 12a
(omitted in his quotation) is itself the content of the foreign
speech, which, because even it will not be heeded, will result in
the judgment and destruction prophesied in verse 13b.

Another question concerns the identity of "some(one) who
do(es) not understand" ("outsider[s]," "uninstructed one[s]")
mentioned in verses 23 and 24. How precisely is the Greek word
(ἰδιώτης) to be translated? Is the word a further description of

"unbeliever(s)" or does it refer to a group distinct from both them and the congregation? In view of such difficulties, then, it is particularly important here to identify those points that are clear and not obscure them by insisting on those about which we cannot be decisive.

To begin with, the place of this passage within the larger flow of the chapter should not be overlooked. Paul continues his concern with the place of tongues in public worship, particularly relative to prophecy. Up to this point he has shown in various ways that uninterpreted tongues have no place in public worship because others in the congregation do not understand, and so the body as a whole is not edified. Now, before laying down guidelines for regulating the use of prophecy and tongues in public worship (vv. 26ff.), he goes on to bring into view unbelievers, those who are not members of the congregation, in relation to tongues (and prophecy). He makes his point(s) by an appeal to the Old Testament, and by contrasting the (hypothetical) situation where all in the congregation speak in (uninterpreted) tongues with one where all prophesy. These verses, it should also be noted, provide the most explicit indication of the purpose of tongues in the entire chapter.

Tongues, Paul says, are a sign for unbelievers (v. 22a). Whether or not he is correcting a misconception among the Corinthians ("tongues are a sign that shows us we are Christians and have the Spirit"), the significance he attributes to tongues as a sign for unbelievers is evidently negative. Tongues are a sign *against* unbelievers. This can be seen (1) in the use of Isaiah 28:11f. to support the character of tongues as a sign. Whatever the answers to the questions noted above concerning this use of Scripture, the unintelligible speech prophesied is within the setting of God's bringing judgment on Judah for its apostasy and unbelief and so an indication of that judgment. (2) In verses 23–25 Paul pointedly excludes a positive or evangelizing role for tongues. Prophecy, not tongues, attracts unbelievers to the gospel and serves to win them for Christ. Tongues only antagonize and create a false impression ("you're out of your mind"). (3) The tone of the introductory admonition in verse 20, too frequently overlooked in discussing this passage, indicates that Paul is about to say something sobering about the use of tongues, something at least that demands discretion and maturity on the part of his readers.

Paul teaches, then, that tongues are a sign of God's judgment. Especially when unintelligible (that is, uninterpreted), they are an indictment against unbelievers. They show God's rejection of those who have rejected him in unbelief and at the same time confirm that unbelief. They are a mark of his turning away and alienation from those who have spurned the plain, intelligible message of the gospel. This is why Paul, while calling attention to this aspect of the gift (vv. 21f.), nonetheless goes on immediately to caution against its use in the presence of unbelievers: uninterpreted tongues can serve only to harden unbelievers in their rejection of the gospel (v. 23), and believers of sound mind (cf. v. 20) will want to have no part in provoking such hardening in those that seek out their gatherings; therefore the exercise of tongues in public worship must be orderly and always interpreted (v. 27). Paul's point is that those who speak in tongues ought always to be aware of what this activity in its function as a sign implies, especially when the gift is used publicly (as it is primarily intended to be). The aspect or function of tongues as a sign also explains their distinctiveness (and apparent cumbersomeness) as a mode of revelation: as the Word of God they are at the same time a sign of his judgment on unbelief.

The character of tongues as a sign, as already noted, is derived by Paul from Isaiah's prophecy of God's impending judgment on unrepentant Judah. How more exactly are we to assess this use of the Old Testament? Just how are tongues related to this prophecy?

Perhaps we should conclude, on the assumption that the prophecy had an immediate fulfillment in the Assyrian and/or Babylonian domination (occupation) of Judah, that Paul is appealing to Isaiah only as an example, as a loose historical analogy which illustrates the fact that God's unintelligible speech displays his judgment on hardened unbelief. Such a use of the Old Testament would be similar to I Corinthians 9:9, where Paul appeals to Deuteronomy 25:4 ("Do not muzzle an ox when it is treading out the grain") to illustrate the general consideration that those who serve are entitled to material support from those served (cf. v. 14).

There are considerations, however, which point to the conclusion that Paul appeals to Isaiah not merely as a historical analogy but as a true prophecy concerning "this people," that is, the Jews, God's old covenant people. Tongues are the ultimate, new covenant fulfillment of this prophecy. As a sign to unbelievers, they bear primarily, although not exclusively, on unrepentant *Israel*. This view is sometimes dismissed as too subtle and contrived. But the grounds for it are not so easily ignored and require that we at least remain open to the live possibility that this is in fact Paul's thought.

1. Earlier we noted the tie between tongues and the parables of Jesus in terms of the common "mystery"-content of both. Jesus' parables are also the closest equivalent elsewhere in the New Testament to tongues as a judgment sign. All four Gospels report teaching of Jesus on the purpose of parables (Matt. 13:10–15; Mark 4:10–12; Luke 8:9f.; cf. John 9:39ff. with 10:6, 19ff., 24): as veiled, indirect speech (see the complaint of the Jews reflected in John 10:24: "... tell us plainly"), parables are in Jesus' hand an instrument of discriminating judgment (cf. John 9:39), addressed to those outside the circle of his disciples (Mark 4:11), which serve either to attract in faith or repel and confirm in unbelief. The Synoptic Gospels accent the negative or hardening side: parables function, in the words and as the fulfillment of Isaiah 6:9, 10, quoted most fully in Matthew, "so that 'in seeing they may see and yet not see, and in hearing may hear and yet not understand, lest they return and be forgiven'" (Mark 4:12). As parables of the *kingdom* of God (e.g., Matt. 13:18f., 24, 31–33), which disclose to the disciples the mysteries of the kingdom (Matt. 13:11) already *present* (e.g., 12:28; 13:16f.), the hardening they also serve is *eschatological*; they bring about a final and decisive rejection of God and his covenant.

This discriminating, judicial function is true of the parables of Jesus. It is not a universal mark of parabolic speech as such to harden or to intensify opposition. What is said of Jesus' use of parables does not apply to parables elsewhere in Scripture or beyond. Ministers of the gospel today, for example, do not seek to imitate Jesus by employing parabolic devices in order that some of their hearers "may hear but not understand." This function of

Jesus' parables is a distinctive mark of his earthly ministry. It is an index of the redemptive-historical context in which "he came to his own, but his own did not receive him" (John 1:11). It is bound up inseparably with the decisive transition from old to new and final in covenant history, a transition which issues in the founding of the church.

Accordingly, Jesus' parables serve to separate faith from unbelief in *Israel*. The unbelief hardened by the veiling speech of his parables is specifically *Jewish* unbelief and covenant unfaithfulness. In a similar way, then, the related phenomenon of (kingdom) mysteries unintelligibly expressed in tongues (cf. I Cor. 14:2), likewise in the context of founding the church, serves to demonstrate God's (new covenant) judgment and rejection of Israel (cf. Rom. 11:15) and so to intensify and harden unbelief that is primarily Jewish.

2. Characteristically, New Testament appeal to the Old is not simply to the words cited but to their larger context. In the instance of Paul's citation of Isaiah 28, verses 11 and 12 are part of the same unit of text as verse 16. The prophecy of the judgment on Judah of strange, foreign speech is of one piece with the prophecy, "Behold, I am laying in Zion a stone, a tested stone, a costly cornerstone for the foundation, firmly placed" (NASB).

In the New Testament this verse is prominent in the church-house passages; it is quoted in I Peter 2:6 (cf. v. 4) and evidently underlies the imagery of Ephesians 2:20 (cf. I Cor. 3:11). Christ as the church's foundation is the fulfillment of this prophecy. But it is also cited in Romans 9:33 (cf. 10:11), where it is applied to the offense taken by unbelieving *Israel* (cf. 9:31f.) at Christ and the gospel. The judgment on Judah foretold by Isaiah, including God's alien speech, is fulfilled by the foundation-laying realized in Christ and the apostles (and prophets). The time of God's (once-for-all) activity of laying a foundation in Zion is also the time of terminal judgment on the unbelief in Zion provoked by that activity. The same combination of God's (foundation) stone and stumbling offense at it is present in Psalm 118:22, 23, and Isaiah 8:14, 15; and in the New Testament both these passages are likewise seen to be fulfilled in the ministry of Christ and the

antagonistic, unbelieving reaction against it that is primarily
Jewish (Matt. 21:42 and parallels; Luke 2:34; Acts 4:11; Rom. 9:32;
cf. I Peter 2:4–8).

Within this larger framework of prophecy and fulfillment, then,
Paul's point in I Corinthians 14:21f. is that tongues are the sign of
God's judgment at the inauguration of the new covenant and the
founding of the church. Tongues are the sign correlative with this
(foundation-laying) activity which occasions (primarily Jewish)
unbelief and the eschatological judgment attendant on it. Tongues
mark the fulfillment of the prophecy, reinforced by Simeon at
Christ's birth, that "this child is destined to cause the falling and
rising of many in Israel, and to be a sign that will be rejected"
(Luke 2:34). There is additional support for this conclusion if, as
some maintain, the Old Testament passages just noted, including
Isaiah 28, are among a collection of *testimonia* used by the early
church in its confrontation with Judaism.

3. The preceding two points may seem to involve a compli-
cated understanding of the passage, which in any case would
have been lost on Paul's Corinthian readers. But these objections
are offset by recalling the background at Corinth. According to the
record in Acts, Jewish opposition to Paul and the gospel, which
was a constant and decisive factor over the course of all three
missionary journeys, was especially rampant at Corinth and as
intense there as anywhere else (Acts 18:1–17). Presumably, unbelief that was primarily, though not exclusively, Jewish was very
much a day-in, day-out reality of which his readers were all too
aware.

Also, the view presented here does not depend on restricting
tongues as a sign to unbelieving Jews. I Corinthians 14:22a applies
to all unbelievers; the foundation of Christ crucified, proclaimed
by the apostles, is not only a stumbling block to the Jews, but fool-
ishness to the Gentiles (I Cor. 1:23). Nonetheless, the fact remains
that it was specifically Jewish unbelief and rejection of Christ that
was decisive for the destruction of the old covenant order and the
laying of the new covenant foundation.

Conclusion: If the preceding discussion correctly analyzes
Paul's intention in these verses, particularly the significance of

his appeal to the Old Testament, then they provide additional support for the conclusion that tongues were a temporary gift which has been withdrawn from the church along with the apostles and prophets. Along with other developments in the foundational and transitional period in covenant history which began with the coming of Christ and ended with the destruction of Jerusalem, tongues were an indication that the kingdom of God had been taken away from hardened, unbelieving Israel and given to a nation producing its fruit (Matt. 21:43; cf. the use of Ps. 118:22 in v. 42 and Deut. 32:21). Further, it should not be overlooked that, whatever the significance of tongues as a sign, Paul clearly teaches that this function as a sign is an integral characteristic of tongues, present wherever the gift is exercised.

E. I Corinthians 13:8–13

This passage, particularly verse 10 ("when the perfect comes, the partial will pass away"), is frequently appealed to as teaching conclusively that prophecy and tongues are to continue in the church until Christ's return. After all else has been said, this passage appears to be the immovable stumbling block for the view that these gifts have ceased.

The coming of "the perfect" (v. 10) and the "then" of the believer's full knowledge (v. 12) no doubt refer to the time of Christ's return. The view that they describe the point at which the New Testament canon is completed cannot be made credible exegetically. While this view rests on the correct insight that prophecy and tongues are tied to the foundational, canon-forming period of the church's history, it strains Paul's statements by reading into them considerations that are outside his scope here. However, the conclusion that this passage teaches the intended continuation of prophecy and tongues until Christ's return is likewise gratuitous and reads Paul too explicitly in terms of the issues raised in the present-day controversy over spiritual gifts. Unlike the Pastoral Epistles, where he makes specific provision for the postapostolic future of the church, Paul is not oriented here to the distinction between the apostolic, foundational present and the period beyond. Rather he has in view the entire period until Christ's return, without regard to whether or not discontinuities may intervene during the course of this period, in the interests of emphasizing the enduring quality of faith, hope, and especially love (vv. 8, 13). As a whole chapter 13 is concerned with the supreme importance of love in the Christian life ("the most excellent way," 12:31b), and with distinguishing love from the various gifts mentioned in chapter 12. Verses 1–3 contrast love with a loveless exercise of these gifts. Verses 4–7 enumerate some of the sterling qualities of love. At verse 8 the discussion is given a new turn in which the dominant, integrating theme through verse 12 is knowledge. Love and the gifts are considered in terms of this theme, and their relationship is set within the contrast between the believer's knowledge at present and after Christ's return (v. 8: " . . . knowledge . . . will pass away"; v. 9: "we know in part"; v. 11: the contrast between childish and adult speaking, thinking, and reasoning; v. 12: the contrast between seeing in a mirror dimly and face to face, between knowing in part and as the believer is fully known). Present knowledge is fragmentary and opaque (vv. 9, 12); the knowledge of the future, consummate, clear, and direct (v. 12). The contrast between "the partial" and "the perfect" (v. 10; cf. vv. 9, 12) is qualitative, not quantitative— between what is constitutive for the present order of things (which is "passing away," cf. 7:31) and the future age in its absoluteness.

Within this framework the gifts are on the side of the believer's present, transient knowledge. The gifts do not of themselves form one side of the contrast but are part of a larger picture. Hence, the specific point of verse 8 ("as for prophecies, they will pass away; as for tongues, they will cease; as for knowledge, it will pass away," RSV) is to stress the temporary and provisional nature not simply of the believer's present knowledge, but, correlatively, of the ways he comes to know. Prophecy and tongues are in view as modes of revelation related to the believer's present knowledge (whether or not "knowledge" in verse 8 is an additional, third gift, parallel with prophecy and tongues). Paul's intention is seen in the progressive simplifying of his focus from prophecy, tongues, and knowledge (v. 8), to prophecy and knowledge (v. 9), to knowledge (vv. 10-12). In contrast to love on the one side, on the other side he moves from revelatory gifts exercised by some in the church to the present knowledge, for which revelation is basic, of *all* believers.

The reason that prophecy and tongues are singled out as modes of revelation is no doubt because of the situation at Corinth addressed in the larger context, and Paul's extensive preoccupation with the proper exercise of these gifts in chapter 14. But this selection must also be assessed in the light of our analysis that at 13:8 the relationship between love and the gifts is taken up into the broader contrast between the believer's present and future knowledge, in which on the one side the primary accent is not on the cessation of particular revelatory gifts but on the temporary and fragmentary character of present knowledge. If this analysis is correct, then it is important to recognize that in terms of his underlying concern with the believer's present knowledge, Paul might well have also mentioned *inscripturation* as a mode of revelation. We frequently overlook that all special revelation, including Scripture (with all its perfections: authority, necessity, sufficiency, clarity), is a "mirror" for the present order of "seeing dimly," a temporary aid which will pass away, along with everything else that constitutes our knowledge here, at the coming of that "seeing," which is "face to face." The Bible on the pulpit is a sign to the congregation that it is a pilgrim congregation, that the church is still a people "on the way."

But inscripturation has ceased. And if that be granted, then it is gratuitous to insist that this passage teaches that the modes of revelation mentioned, prophecy and tongues, are to continue functioning in the church until Christ's return. Paul is not intending to specify the time when any particular mode will cease. What he does affirm is the termination of the believer's present, fragmentary knowledge, based on likewise temporary modes of revelation, when "the perfect" comes. The time of the cessation of prophecy and tongues is an open question so far as this passage is concerned and will have to be decided on the basis of other passages and considerations.

Before leaving this passage we can note briefly the bearing of the preceding discussion on the concluding statement in verse 13 and the perennial difficulty many have had with how faith and hope can be said to abide beyond Christ's return. Probably Paul is not saying that they will continue to function in some way after Christ returns, although that position is defensible. Rather, in view of his immediately preceding focus on knowledge, his point seems to be that faith, hope, and love "reach ahead" of the believer's present knowledge, particularly in its character as "sight" (v. 12a), not because they are divorced from that knowledge or directed by some noncognitive principle, but because they grasp and anticipate, in a way our present knowledge (along with whatever spiritual gifts we have) does not, the perfection of the order introduced at Christ's return. This eschatological "reach," in contrast to the believer's present "sight," is indicated elsewhere: for faith in II Corinthians 5:7 ("we walk by faith, not by sight"), for hope in Romans 8:24, 25 ("hope that is seen is not hope," "we hope for what we do not see"), for love and faith in I Peter 1:8 ("though you have not seen him, you love him; and even though you do not see him now, you believe in him," NIV). Note also the related contrast between love and the believer's present knowledge, whether rightly or wrongly utilized, which structures I Corinthians 8 in its entirety.

F. The Question of Cessation in General

How, in general, are we to determine what activities of the Spirit are intended only for the foundational period of the church and what activities continue beyond? In the first place, the answer does not lie in a quasi-mechanical distinguishing (within the lists of Romans 12, I Corinthians 12, and Ephesians 4) between extraordinary gifts that have ceased and ordinary gifts that continue or, what would be worse, between supernatural and natural gifts. Such an approach involves a much too inorganic handling of Scripture. I Corinthians 12:12–27 and Romans 12:4, 5 especially make clear that the gifts mentioned in these lists are organically interrelated in their functioning. As such they are, in turn, an integral part of a living church situation, a church situation which as a *whole,* then, is in certain respects discontinuous with postapostolic conditions.

Within the overall, unified composition of the New Testament, the Pastoral Epistles, most prominently, address and make specific provision for our postapostolic church situation, in distinction from the situation we find, say, in the major letters of Paul. The balance of continuities and discontinuities between the two situations is largely to be identified from the picture brought into view in the Pastorals. The directions given there for the life of the church and the ordering of its ministry, together with the basic perspectives spelled out above in chapter III, provide general guidelines for determining the gifts and ministries intended for the church today. So far as *word*-gifts that continue are concerned, the governing principle is "the Spirit with the word": the Spirit working in a convicting and illuminating fashion with the foundational, apostolic tradition or deposit (II Thess. 2:15; 3:6; I Tim. 6:20; II Tim. 1:12, 14), and so eventually with the completed canon.

G. Healing and Related Gifts

In this and the preceding chapters we have been occupied almost exclusively with prophecy and tongues, and the question of their cessation. Almost as prominent today is an interest in healing and similar "spectacular" gifts. How do our findings so far in this study bear on the question of these gifts and their place in the life of the church?

Briefly, healing and related gifts stand in a different light than *word*-gifts, like prophecy and tongues. They present a somewhat different state of affairs, because they do not raise the issue of revelation and the source(s) of God's Word for the church. Probably, the conclusion to be drawn is that as listed in I Corinthians 12 (vv. 9f., 29f.) and encountered throughout the narrative in Acts, these gifts, particularly when exercised regularly by a given individual, are part of the foundational structure of the church. They are among the "signs of the apostle" in the broader sense indicated above (C.4) and so have passed out of the life of the church. Contemporary ministries of healing and claims to the gift, however else they are to be assessed, are hardly of the same magnitude of unambiguous and sovereign power displayed in the healing miracles of Jesus and the apostles (cf., e.g., Matt. 4:23f.; Luke 8:43f.; John 11:43f.; Acts 5:15f.; 19:11f.). Only the most charitable and undiscerning frame of mind will be able to credit the former as the "greater works" Jesus promised his disciples would do because he was about to go to the Father (John 14:12). (This promise almost certainly refers to the worldwide harvesting of the nations with the gospel, to be accomplished after the ascension and sending of the Spirit; cf. John 4:34–38.)

At the same time, however, the sovereign will and power of God today to heal the sick, particularly in response to prayer (see, e.g., James 5:14, 15), ought to be acknowledged and insisted on. There is nothing in Scripture, certainly nothing this study has brought to light, which would cause us to do anything else than maintain that healing, no matter how hopeless and terminal the prognosis medically, is a reality that has continued in the church's history down to the present, and ought to be an expectation of God's people today. Here, too, our God is "able to do far more abundantly than all that we ask or think, according to the power that works within us" (Eph. 3:20).

But, having emphasized this, we must make one absolutely vital qualification. That God can and does heal disease judged incurable by modern medicine does not mean his will is that all or even some large percentage of such sickness be healed. In such a view faith is inevitably forced into abnormal prominence. The faith of the person seeking to be healed becomes the finally decisive consideration, and success (or failure) depends solely on the strength (or weakness) of his faith. Such a view both fails to reckon with the intended role of severe illness in the life of the believer, and misses the true character of faith.

The experience of Paul himself recounted in II Corinthians 12:7–9 is most instructive in this respect:

> To keep me from becoming conceited because of these surpassingly great revelations, there was given me a thorn in my flesh,

a messenger of Satan, to torment me. Three times I pleaded with the Lord to take it away from me. But he said to me, "My grace is sufficient for you, for my power is made perfect in weakness." Therefore, I will boast all the more gladly about my weaknesses, so that Christ's power may rest on me. (NIV)

While the exact identification of Paul's "thorn in the flesh" continues to be one of the celebrated puzzles of New Testament interpretation, it was almost certainly some kind of illness or physical affliction. It was a chronic and painful affliction. The latter especially is suggested by the image of a sharp thorn embedded in the flesh and by the description of its effect with the strong word "torment" ("beat"). This affliction is further described as a "messenger of Satan," indicating Satan as the source of disease and suffering (cf. Luke 13:16); yet at the same time it is sent ("given") by God.

Paul says that he begged the Lord "three times" to be released from this affliction. Many older exegetes (e.g., Calvin) took this expression as a figure of speech to mean that Paul prayed repeatedly or extensively. Even if it is to be understood literally, it certainly does not have the force of "only three times" or indicate vacillation or halfheartedness in prayer on Paul's part. The agonizing of Jesus' threefold praying in Gethsemane inevitably comes to mind (Matt. 26:44). Coupled with the verb here "three times" suggests intense and repeated prayer. Paul sought the Lord wholeheartedly for deliverance. Yet the Lord did not grant Paul's petition. This was not for negative reasons like doubt or some other flaw in his faith—all indications in the passage are to the contrary—but because of entirely positive considerations: that Christ's grace might prove sufficient and his power be perfected in Paul's weakened condition, and that Paul might be kept from pride and a sense of self-sufficiency. (Cf. Gal. 4:12ff., where Paul indicates that an illness was the occasion of his preaching the gospel to the Galatians for the first time.)

This experience of Paul is certainly bound up with the unique revelations received by him as an apostle (v. 7; cf. vv. 1ff.). However, there is no good reason to doubt that the function of his "thorn in the flesh" serves as a paradigm for physical suffering in

the lives of all Christians. Facile slogans like "healing is for today" and "God desires that all disease be healed" are not only
superficial distortions of biblical teaching, which can wreak
havoc with the faith of those already grievously tried by pain and
suffering. By the confusion such views create they also deprive
believers of one of the great blessings God has for his people in
times of distress, including physical affliction—the blessing of
learning by experience what Paul discovered: "When I am weak,
then I am strong" (II Cor. 12:10).

VI

Quenching the Spirit?

Prophecy and tongues, we have concluded, are revelatory gifts, temporarily given to the church during its foundational, apostolic era. They are inseparably connected with the ministry of the apostles and have since been permanently withdrawn, along with the apostles, from the life of the church.

For many this conclusion is not only plainly wrong but offensive. To them it betrays inexcusable blindness to what they are convinced is incontestable evidence of a new and mighty working of the Holy Spirit in our day; to them we are guilty of trampling underfoot experiences precious to literally millions of Christians around the world. Is it conceivable that so many Christians are wrong? What in fact is to be said about these widespread contemporary claims to have received these New Testament gifts?

These questions (and the controversy surrounding them) can hardly be suppressed or ignored for very long. They demand convincing and constructive answers. They also deserve more attention than will be given to them here. I do little more than mention briefly several key points, hoping at the same time to clear away certain misconceptions that may have resulted along the way.

1. It ought to go without saying that what is usually termed the charismatic movement embodies the concerns and experiences of those who, for the most part, belong to Christ. The differences between charismatics and noncharismatics (to continue using the customary distinctions, which I have called into question on biblical grounds; see above, pp. 46–48), are largely differences between *believers*, differences *within* the one church of Christ. Lamentable is the position taken by some noncharismatics, that since distinctive charismatic experience is not what it claims to be, it must all result from the indwelling influence of Satan or demons. Such an attitude is even more deplorable than the second-blessing sense of superiority sometimes displayed by charismatics; it is not only without warrant biblically, but also escalates divisions and tensions to the point where resolution through mutual *Christian* concern is made virtually impossible. The issue here is the unity and welfare of Christ's *entire* body and the health of *all* its members, both charismatic and noncharismatics (cf. I Cor. 12:26a).

Surely it is not difficult to anticipate what would be among Paul's first words at this point: if I speak the truth of Scripture, but have not love, I am nothing; and if I have all biblical insight and all ability to perceive and point out doctrinal error, but have not love, it profits me (or anyone else) nothing.

2. But while mutual Christian love and concern between charismatics and noncharismatics are indispensable, it ought at the same time to be obvious that such loving concern does not ignore or set aside Scripture. Such a concern depends on Scripture alone for its substance; it is of the Spirit only as it is according to the Word.

One frequently voiced objection to the view that tongues and prophecy have ceased is that it denies the *freedom* of the Holy Spirit ("puts the Spirit in the confining box of our limited theologies") and conflicts with the biblical teaching that the Spirit distributes gifts "just as he wills" (I Cor. 12:11). The weight of this objection is more apparent than real. At issue here is not the sovereign right and power of the Spirit to do what he pleases, but the pattern by which God chooses to reveal his Word to the church, the *structure* or *order* which the Spirit has set for himself in his *freedom*.

No doubt the Spirit is like the wind, which "blows wherever it pleases" (John 3:8); much about his working we find incalculable and mysterious. As the Spirit of the living God, truly his ways are higher than our ways, and his thoughts than our thoughts, just as the heavens are higher than the earth (Isa. 55:9). But the impenetrability and incomprehensibility of the Spirit's work must never be stressed one-sidedly or absolutized, so that the bounds to his revealing activity, definitely indicated by the Spirit himself in Scripture, are obscured or denied. Those bounds, as I have tried to show, provide the church with a foundational, apostolic revelation, adequate and complete for every need and blessing, permitting no additions, until Christ's return—an event which when it takes place *with its precursors*, the New Testament suggests, will *not* be the occasion for widespread division and uncertainty within the church about whether or not it has occurred. The fact that these bounds to the Spirit's revealing work are denied or implicitly questioned by the experience of a large number of contemporary Christians no more proves them nonexistent than the reigning Christianity of his day showed Luther to be wrong.

Reference to Luther at this point is anything but arbitrary. Developments at the time of the Reformation contain a permanent and important lesson, which also bears on the issues raised by the charismatic movement. The extensive writings of both Luther and Calvin, taken as a whole, wage a two-front war. Not only are they directed against Roman Catholicism but also against the "left wing" of the Reformation (Luther: the "enthusiasts," "heavenly prophets"; Calvin: "fanatics," "free spirits"). This "left wing," Anabaptist reaction, quite varied within itself in many respects, nevertheless as a whole was characterized by an emphasis on the Holy Spirit in marked continuity with today's charismatic movement.

The Reformers asserted themselves so energetically on both these fronts, because they recognized that, along with all the obvious differences between the two, they posed a *common* threat to the supremacy of the Bible (*scriptura sola*): Rome with its institutionalized, ecclesiastically authorized body of tradition; the Anabaptists with their spontaneous, charismatically sanctioned "revelations," each endangering the sole authority and sufficiency of Scripture and so the true freedom of the Christian man.

Confirmation of these observations would seem to be found in the way contemporary Roman Catholicism has so easily accommodated the charismatic movement.

3. To conclude, then, that the gifts of prophecy and tongues have been withdrawn from the church is not to be "against the Holy Spirit" or to quench the freedom of the Spirit, but to respect the way in which the Spirit has sovereignly chosen to reveal the will of God and so insure the freedom of the believer. If this is true, then it follows that the charismatic movement needs to reevaluate its distinctive emphases. It ought at least to consider that the best case exegetically for these emphases has probably already been made, and that it is served by theologies that in important respects are not taught in Scripture.

What explanation, then, is to be given for distinctive charismatic experience? This raises a large and complex question. But surely an important step toward arriving at a constructive answer would be for all "sides" in the church to recognize that the Bible does not teach Holy Spirit baptism as a distinct, postconversion experience, and that contemporary charismatic phenomena are not the New Testament gifts of prophecy and tongues.

This is not, as it might at first seem, to demand the "capitulation" of the charismatic movement, or to insist that distinctive charismatic experience is devoid of the Spirit's working. Often what is viewed as postconversion baptism with the Spirit is a misunderstanding of a genuine work of the Spirit, of a particularly decisive or intense experience of his continuing activity in the believer that produces, sometimes suddenly or dramatically, a deepened sense of God's love and renewed confidence, assurance, and joy in Christian living. Often, too, what is seen as prophecy is actually a spontaneous, Spirit-worked application of Scripture, a more or less sudden grasp of the bearing that biblical teaching has on a particular situation or problem. All Christians need to be open to these more spontaneous workings of the Spirit.

On the other hand, there can be no place in the church for the doctrine of postconversion Spirit baptism which, all too frequently, functions in a way that gravely obscures or even denies the fulness and finality of the salvation in Christ received by all believers through faith, as well as the character of that faith as wrought by God's sovereign grace. And alleged prophecies that involve specific guidance and predictions dangerously disregard and undermine the sufficiency of Scripture.

The clear distance between contemporary tongues-phenomena and the New Testament gift can be seen from a number of angles. To mention just several of these again, (1) the contemporary phenomenon is usually viewed as a gift (ideally) for all believers; (2) contemporary tongues are predominantly, if not exclusively, for private devotional use; (3) little, if any, recognition is given to tongues as a sign of judgment against unbelievers; (4) interpretation is either neglected or applied in a dubious fashion. Contemporary tongues are not the gift of the Spirit described in Acts 2 and I Corinthians 12–14.

It ought not simply to be assumed, however, that there is no biblical rationale and support for this contemporary practice and the sense of release and intense, deepened fellowship with God that is often said to accompany it. There is an increasing recognition today, within as well as outside charismatic circles, that spontaneous, nonconceptual free vocalization is a virtually universal human capacity. Is there perhaps a legitimate place for "Christian free vocalization"? This, in my judgment, raises a question that puts the contemporary debate over tongues where it belongs—within the area of worship and of what the Scriptures teach about the way God desires to be worshiped, both corporately and in private. The issue that needs to be explored is the compatibility of nonconceptual vocalization with the regulative principle of worship. To do that here, however, would take us beyond the limits of this study.

4. Many others have already pointed out the unquestionably positive aspects of the charismatic movement: belief in the Holy Spirit as a powerfully present reality, not just a doctrine, protest against intellectualism in theology and formalism in the worship and life of the church, intense prayer and praise, stress on cultivating relationships among believers and a more intimate fellowship within the church. In these and other concerns charismatic Christians challenge the entire church with the need for

searching attention to worship and congregational life that minister to the *whole* believer and involve *all* believers.

But it would be a great loss if the renewed interest of our day in the work of the Holy Spirit were to be expended on the differences between charismatics and noncharismatics, real and important as those differences are. The pressing and promising task before the church today is to demonstrate unambiguously, in practice as well as proclamation, that at its *core* the gospel concerns not only the free and full remission of sin but the present reality of a new creation and eschatological life in Christ, the present renewal and transformation of the believer in his entirety, according to the inner man, and the redirection and reintegration of human life in all its aspects.

The gospel is the gospel of the exalted Christ, the life-giving Spirit. This is one perspective on Pentecost the church cannot afford to lose. Without it the church will be uncertain of itself and ineffective in serving its Lord; with this perspective it is more than equal to its mission in the world. In the "firstfruits" power of Pentecost the church lives eloquently in hope of the glory to be revealed (Rom. 8:18–25), confident in its expectation of a new heaven and a new earth in which righteousness dwells (II Peter 3:13).

Scripture Index